The Snare of Indifference

Lukewarmness

Archbishop Nicholas Duncan-Williams

Copyright © 2023 by Nicholas Duncan-Williams

All rights reserved.

No part of this book may be reproduced in any form or by any electronic or mechanical means, including information storage and retrieval systems, without written permission from the author, except for the use of brief quotations in a book review.

Contents

Introduction	v
1. Lukewarmness: A Silent Threat to Our Spiritual Lives	1
2. The Fiery Passion or the Chilling Apathy?	9
3. Beware of the End Time Lukewarmness	20
4. Don't Die a Slow Spiritual Death	37
5. The Necessity of Christian Fellowship	52
6. Pleasing People: A Hidden Trap for Believers	59
7. Why that Appetite for Worldliness?	73
8. Watch These Killer Attitudes	82
9. Walk in the Zeal of the Lord	93
Epilogue	109
About the Author	113

Introduction

In the depths of my memories, I journey back to the days of being born again, when the flame of devotion ignited within us, and we found solace in the sanctuary of the church.

Oh, how those moments flood my mind and heart with a refreshing nostalgia! Among them, Friday nights stand tall as pillars of fervor and anticipation, for it was on those hallowed nights that our spirits soared.

Sleep eluded us as we eagerly ventured into the embrace of the church, our souls ablaze with anticipation. The air crackled with electric energy, charged with the fervent prayers that echoed through the sanctuary. In that sacred space, we would bend and stretch the limits of our faith, yearning to draw closer to God. Ah, the all-night prayer vigils of yesteryears, where countless souls found their fervor, purpose, and destiny.

And who could forget the cherished bible studies, those sacred gatherings where we hungered for the Word of God, where we sought to nourish our souls and deepen our commu-

Introduction

nion with God? We arrived with hearts and minds prepared, eager to receive the pearls of wisdom that would illuminate our paths. Our thirst for understanding, for a profound connection with the Holy Spirit, propelled us forward on this spiritual journey.

We were a tapestry of dedication, intricately woven into the fabric of our home cells, embracing every aspect of communal life in the church. Our commitment knew no bounds, and we embraced every opportunity to serve and uplift our brethren. Questions were silenced, doubts cast aside, for we were consumed by a love for the church, an unyielding desire to be an integral part of the tapestry of the Body of Christ.

Alas, the passage of time, like a silent thief, has wrought changes upon the landscape of the devotion of the people of God. I see it now, a gradual decline seeping into the very essence of commitment, love for God, and love for one another. The fervor that once set hearts ablaze has waned, and the bond of fellowship grows fragile. It is as if the foundations of faith have crumbled, leaving fragments of confusion and disillusionment in their wake.

Yet, amidst the disarray and the pieces that no longer fit, a great hope remains. For just as time has eroded devotion, it can also be the catalyst for renewal. Let us remember the fervor of those bygone days and kindle the flame that once burned brightly. Let us reclaim the unity that made us strong and reforge the bonds of fellowship that have frayed.

We find ourselves at a crossroads in this dance of faith and humanity. Shall we allow the decline to consume the people of God, or shall we rise, rejuvenate, and breathe life back into the sacred spaces we have neglected? The choice is yours to make,

Introduction

for even amidst the disarray, the yearning for connection still stirs within the souls of us all. May we heed its call, reclaim the fervor of our youth, and rebuild a sanctuary of love, devotion, and purpose once more.

In the vast expanse of time spanning two millennia, the church has traversed various stages, mirroring the seven churches immortalized in the sacred verses of the Book of Revelations, penned by the hand of John as delivered to him by our Lord Jesus Christ.

Yet, as I cast my discerning gaze upon the present state of our congregations, the very essence of our actions reverberates with profound meaning. The once vibrant applause has dwindled, subdued by a pervasive apathy. The souls adorning the pews sit adrift, their minds drifting far from the sacred ministry unfolding before them. Like lost souls, they meander through the hallowed halls of defiance, their hearts frozen, devoid of fervor. An unsettling dissonance permeates the air, for something is awry.

Compelled by an insatiable thirst for understanding, I delve deep into the sacred pages of the Book of Revelation, where a revelation within the revelation begins to unfurl its enigmatic tapestry. Behold, the state of the modern church aligns with the seventh church depicted in the Biblical text, bearing the scars and countenance of its predecessors. Evident are the telltale signs, marking the precipice of the last days or perchance, already crossing that somber threshold.

Within these signs lie cryptic messages that demand our unwavering attention, for they wield great power over our spiritual existence. As believers, we are summoned to rise from the depths of our indifference, embrace the transformative winds of change, and realign ourselves with the timeless truths of God's Word.

Even as the Master's voice resounds, proclaiming, *"To him that overcometh will I not blot out his name from the book of life,"* the weight of His words falls not upon the unbeliever but upon the souls reborn, vessels sanctified by the indwelling of the Holy Spirit, redeemed through the precious sacrifice of Christ's blood. Thus, we are implored to conquer the adversities that assail our faith, lest our names be forever erased from the eternal ledger of life.

And in the sacred annals of Matthew 24:13, the Savior's voice echoes through the corridors of time, declaring, *"He that endureth to the end shall be saved."* Salvation, though a glorious beginning, unveils its true splendor when it permeates every fiber of our being and when our devotion endures the trials and tribulations that test our resolve.

My purpose remains unwavering within the sacred verses of the Book of Revelation, a tapestry woven with prophetic visions of the world's end. I endeavor to illuminate a critical sign, often overlooked yet capable of insidiously eroding the steadfastness of believers in Christ. Let us embark, then, upon this perilous journey into the realm of lukewarmness, an insidious state that demands our immediate attention.

Though it beckons us to embrace complacency, I beseech you, dear family of God, to rouse the dormant embers within your spirits. Remain vigilant, for within lies the key to unlocking the doors of our spiritual destinies. Let humility guide our steps as we traverse this treacherous path, firmly clasping the timeless truths that shall shape our eternal testimonies before God.

For within the treacherous chasms of lukewarmness, souls

Introduction

teeter on the precipice of danger, foundations crumble beneath their weight, and purpose flounders in the shadows. Only by heeding the resounding clarion call can we rekindle the flame of devotion, casting off the shackles of indifference and embracing the fervor of authentic discipleship. Let our hearts ignite with the zeal befitting those who tread the narrow path.

Chapter 1

Lukewarmness: A Silent Threat to Our Spiritual Lives

A lukewarm Christian is much like a cup of lukewarm coffee; neither hot nor cold, they don't really seem to benefit anyone. - E. Stanley Jones

In the depths of my being, a fervent passion burns for the imminent return of our Lord Jesus Christ to this earthly realm.

As I reflect upon the pivotal moments leading up to His crucifixion, I am reminded of the profound conversation He shared with His disciples—a conversation that sought to allay their fears and impart a renewed sense of hope amidst the challenges ahead. It is within this dialogue that He spoke these resolute words:

"Let not your heart be troubled; you believe in God, believe also in Me. In My Father's house are many mansions; if it were not so, I would have told you. I go to prepare a place for you. And if I

go and prepare a place for you, I will come again and receive you to Myself; that where I am, there you may be also. And where I go you know, and the way you know." John 14:1-4

In these profound declarations, Jesus unveiled the grand tapestry of the future—His journey to the cross, His victorious resurrection, His glorious ascension, and His promised return.

These words, uttered by the very lips of our Lord, resound with absolute authority and certainty. They leave no room for human debate or skepticism. The Second Coming of Jesus Christ is an event poised to unfold, an event meticulously ordained long before the foundation of the world, even alluded to in the earliest pages of Genesis.

What distinguishes this momentous occasion is its significance—a divine continuation and culmination of the original agenda set forth when the Word became Flesh and dwelt among us. Under the dispensation of the Incarnate Word, humanity was offered the opportunity to reshape its understanding, to embrace a more intimate and accurate knowledge of God than ever before.

The heart of this divine agenda beats with the resounding truth that God is our Father, eagerly yearning for the return of His lost children to the warmth of His embrace.

But as the ages have unfolded, a pervasive spiritual malaise has swept over the church—a dangerous state of lukewarmness that threatens to dull our hearts, obscure our vision, and hinder our preparedness for the coming of our King.

It is this lukewarmness, this complacency, that compels me to pen these words—to awaken souls to the urgency of Christ's Second Coming, to ignite a fire within each believer's heart, and to offer guidance on how to overcome the perils of lukewarmness that may hinder our spiritual journey.

In the following pages, we will embark on a transformative exploration that delves into the depths of Scripture, unravels the signs of the times, and beckons believers to rise from the slumber of lukewarmness. Together, we will kindle hope, renew faith, and embrace the imminent return of our Lord Jesus Christ with fervor, devotion, and unwavering anticipation.

For in the wake of lukewarmness lies the promise of renewal, the call to righteousness, and the glorious anticipation of our eternal destiny. So let us journey together, awakening to His return, overcoming lukewarmness, and embracing the radiant dawn of His coming Kingdom.

In the grand tapestry of God's redemptive plan, the incarnation of the Word held a twofold agenda—one to offer the sons of men an opportunity for reconciliation with their Creator and the other to herald a great harvest of souls.

As the echoes of Adam's fall reverberated through the corridors of time, humanity was gripped by the despairing grip of sin and its inevitable consequence—eternal separation from God. Yet, in His boundless love and mercy, God crafted a divine plan that would restore the shattered fellowship between Himself and His creation.

Under the dispensation of the Word made Flesh, a profound shift occurred. Humanity was granted the privilege of receiving forgiveness, cleansing, and restoration to the original intimacy in the early moments of life on earth.

Through the sacrifice of Jesus Christ, the opportunity for reconciliation with God was made accessible to all who would believe and embrace the gift of abundant life.

However, this Second Coming of Jesus Christ, foretold by the Lord Himself, bears a distinct purpose—gathering the harvest. When Jesus spoke of the plenteous harvest and the scarcity of laborers, He illuminated the staggering reality that multitudes still reside outside the heavenly realm.

Millions have yet to encounter the heavenly Father who passionately seeks His lost children, even going to the extent of descending in human form through His Son, Jesus Christ, to seek and save them.

The Second Coming signifies the culmination of this harvest—an event that has been over two millennia in the making. Though shorter in duration than the time between the prophecy of the Seed of the Woman and His triumphant arrival, humanity's propensity for impatience has led some to disregard or even dismiss the reality of Christ's return.

God anticipated this response in His divine wisdom and inspired the Apostle Peter to deliver a solemn warning and affirmation of truth regarding the Second Coming. Peter's words echo through the ages, serving as an alert to humanity's scoffers and a reaffirmation of God's faithfulness.

> *3 knowing this first: that scoffers will come in the last days, walking according to their own lusts, 4 and saying, "Where is the promise of His coming? For since the fathers fell asleep, all things continue as they were from the beginning of creation." 5 For this they willfully forget: that by the word of God the heavens were of old, and the earth standing out of water and in the water,*
>
> *8 But, beloved, do not forget this one thing, that with the Lord one day is as a thousand years, and a thousand years as one*

day. [9] The Lord is not slack concerning His promise, as some count slackness, but is longsuffering toward us, not willing that any should perish but that all should come to repentance. [10] But the day of the Lord will come as a thief in the night, in which the heavens will pass away with a great noise, and the elements will melt with fervent heat; both the earth and the works that are in it will be burned up. [11] Therefore, since all these things will be dissolved, what manner of persons ought you to be in holy conduct and Godliness, [12] looking for and hastening the coming of the day of God, because of which the heavens will be dissolved, being on fire, and the elements will melt with fervent heat? [13] Nevertheless we, according to His promise, look for new heavens and a new earth in which righteousness dwells. 2 Peter 3:3-5, 8-10

As we ponder the passage from 2 Peter 3, we realize that the promise of Christ's return remains a topic sorely neglected in our contemporary pulpits and Christian spaces.

The urgency of His imminent arrival seems to have been muted, overshadowed by the distractions and pursuits of this present age. Yet, the Scriptures resound with unwavering clarity —a reminder that the day of the Lord will come like a thief in the night, shattering the heavens and earth with fervent heat.

In light of these truths, we are compelled to examine our lives and consider the implications of the approaching day of God. It is a call to holy conduct and godliness, a summons to be watchful and eagerly anticipate the consummation of all things in new heavens and a new earth where righteousness shall dwell.

Together, let us reclaim the urgency of the Second Coming,

ignite the revival fires, and prepare ourselves as laborers for the harvest that awaits. For in anticipation of Christ's return lies the hope of reconciliation, the promise of revival, and the glorious culmination of God's divine plan.

In the revival that swept across my beloved country, Ghana, in the late 60s and throughout the 70s, a fervent wave of spiritual awakening engulfed the nation. Christian fellowships sprouted like blooming flowers, and it was during this period that most of the charismatic churches were established.

In the hearts of believers, the theme of the Second Coming burned brightly, its flames illuminating their lives. Messages of Christ's imminent return and teachings on the end times saturated the Christian space. As a result, people lived with a sense of urgency, their hearts aflame and their spirits ready for His glorious arrival.

But alas, the picture has changed over time. In particular, the Charismatic church, over the past 50 years, has shifted its focus towards living a comfortable and prosperous life in the present.

The message of material abundance, while rooted in the truth that God desires His children to live in abundance, has overshadowed any mention of the future and, most significantly, the Second Coming of Christ.

The church finds itself at a self-imposed crossroads, faced with the decision of reclaiming the theme of His return and allowing it to permeate our spiritual realm once again or succumbing to the temptation of offering solace and hope solely for a blissful earthly existence, devoid of any consideration of what lies ahead.

The Snare of Indifference

The once-pervasive attitude of urgency towards the Second Coming has given way to a prevailing attitude of lukewarmness.

In his first epistle, the Apostle John eloquently addresses the glorious prospect of Jesus' Coming. He highlights the astounding love bestowed upon us by the Father, transforming us into His beloved children.

> *Behold what manner of love the Father has bestowed on us, that we should be called children of God! Therefore, the world does not know us, because it did not know Him. ² Beloved, now we are children of God; and it has not yet been revealed what we shall be, but we know that when He is revealed, we shall be like Him, for we shall see Him as He is. ³ And everyone who has this hope in Him purifies himself, just as He is pure.* 1 John 3:1-3

The world may fail to recognize us, for it failed to recognize Him, but we, as believers, are now children of God. Although the full extent of what we shall become has not yet been unveiled, we know that we shall be like Him when He is revealed, for we shall see Him as He truly is. This hope, firmly rooted in our hearts, compels us to purify ourselves, just as He is pure.

John's words resound with the echo of the Apostle Peter's message, resonating through the ages.

As we anticipate the dissolution of this earthly realm to make way for the new, we are confronted with a profound question: What manner of persons ought we to be in our conduct and devotion to God?

Living in earnest expectation of His imminent return demands nothing less than an unwavering commitment to holy living and a fervent passion for the kingdom of God. There is no room for complacency or apathy in the hearts of those eagerly awaiting His arrival.

Conversely, those who fail to grasp the gravity and reality of the Second Coming find themselves drifting towards lukewarmness. The absence of passion and commitment towards this imminent event stifles the flames of devotion, leaving them neither hot nor cold.

Each of us must make a deliberate choice regarding this matter, for the words spoken by Jesus Himself 2000 years ago are as true today as they were then.

Let us not forget, even if the Second Coming does not stir a passionate fire within your heart, that the inevitability of death looms over us all.

In the face of this reality, the question remains: Were you a fervent and zealous follower of Christ during your earthly sojourn, or were you cold and indifferent, or worse still, caught in the lukewarm realm of mediocrity?

The implications are profound, my dear friends. The call to reject lukewarmness and embrace the fervor of anticipation should resound in the depths of our souls. So may we be reminded that our time on this earthly plane is transient, and the time is short for the Lord's return is near.

Chapter 2

The Fiery Passion or the Chilling Apathy?

If you are not as close to God as you used to be, who moved? -
Unknown

Amidst the shifting tides of these end times, we find ourselves confronted with a profound question—one that echoes through the corridors of eternity. To explore this question, let us turn our gaze to the words of Jesus, as recorded in the Book of Revelation.

14 "And to the angel of the church of the Laodiceans write, 'These things says the Amen, the Faithful and True Witness, the Beginning of the creation of God:

15 "I know your works, that you are neither cold nor hot. I could wish you were cold or hot. 16 So then, because you are lukewarm, and neither cold nor hot, I will vomit you out of My mouth.

17 Because you say, 'I am rich, have become wealthy, and

> have need of nothing'—and do not know that you are wretched, miserable, poor, blind, and naked—
>
> *18* I counsel you to buy from Me gold refined in the fire, that you may be rich; and white garments, that you may be clothed, that the shame of your nakedness may not be revealed; and anoint your eyes with eye salve, that you may see.
>
> *19* As many as I love, I rebuke and chasten. Therefore, be zealous and repent.
>
> *20* Behold, I stand at the door and knock. If anyone hears My voice and opens the door, I will come in to him and dine with him, and he with Me. Revelation 3:14-20

These verses unveil a pivotal truth, encapsulating the essence of our spiritual condition in a world veiled by shadows. This divine revelation, intended for believers of our time, speaks directly to our hearts and souls.

For we are the chosen ones, dwelling in the very twilight of humanity's journey. Every word contained within these sacred verses serves as a guiding light, illuminating our path toward eternity. It is within our grasp to shape our destiny and partake in the eternal blessings God has lovingly prepared for His faithful children.

In this passage, Jesus draws a distinction—a divine demarcation—between two types of believers: the fervently passionate and the frigidly indifferent. He unveils the truth of what it means to be hot or cold in the eyes of our Lord. So, who truly embodies the fiery passion of the hot Christian, and who, then, personifies the icy apathy of the cold Christian?

Imagine the essence of heat—an intense energy radiating from a source, engulfing all in its path with its transformative power. It warms, illuminates, and leaves an indelible mark on everything it encounters.

The hot Christian mirrors this very essence. They exude a passionate fervor, an unwavering dedication that touches the lives of those around them. Their faith is not confined to mere words but is a force that ignites souls and imparts life-giving warmth to a world in desperate need.

In stark contrast, consider the chilling touch of coldness. It freezes and stagnates, robbing life of its vitality. The cold Christian, devoid of spiritual fervor, fails to kindle the flame within their own heart, let alone the hearts of others.

They withhold the very essence of life, leaving those who cross their path in a state of spiritual inertia and paralysis. Coldness numbs, freezes, and halts the flow of divine energy.

A Deeper Look

Let us delve deeper into the implications of Jesus' words, seeking a clearer understanding of His expectations for His followers. A believer who burns with the fire of God within their heart embodies the essence of a hot Christian. Their love for the Lord is unwavering, their passion for His Kingdom consuming their very being.

They cannot contain the joy and truth they have found in Jesus, and their life becomes a vibrant testimony of God's transforming power. Unashamed, they boldly proclaim their faith, infecting those around them with their contagious passion for God.

They are a radiant light shining forth in a world desperate

for hope. Their words and actions bear witness to the life and light of God, illuminating every corner they traverse.

Yet, we must address the misconception that Jesus endorses coldness in this context. He states, "I would that you were either cold or hot."

However, Jesus is not suggesting that cold is acceptable or preferable. Instead, he presents a contrast between the two extremes to emphasize the dangers of lukewarmness. He desires fervency and devotion from His followers, and lukewarmness falls short of His standard.

To be lukewarm is to dwell in a state of uncertainty, straddling the line between commitment and indifference. It is to be unpredictable in one's faith, displaying inconsistency and unreliability.

Lukewarmness hinders a believer's impact on the world, for it obscures the reflection of Christ within them. Jesus longs for believers on fire for Him, whose lives consistently mirror His love and truth.

Consider the practical implications of lukewarmness. It breeds unpredictability, causing confusion and disappointment among those who observe our lives. Just as you cannot plan or rely on someone inconsistent and unpredictable, a lukewarm believer's actions and words become a source of uncertainty.

Lukewarmness disappoints both Jesus and those who expect to witness the transformative power of His presence within us.

Jesus, in His divine wisdom, expresses His preference for hot or cold believers. His desire for transparency and devotion stems from His perfect knowledge of our hearts. While His words may seem akin to human expectations, we must remember that Jesus knows us intimately and desires the best for us.

In the broader context of the Book of Revelation, Jesus speaks of His imminent return to the earth. His words carry weight as He warns against lukewarmness in the face of the end times. It is in this context that we must interpret His preference for hot believers. He desires faithful and devoted people, prepared to meet Him upon His return.

Let us, therefore, heed His words and examine our own hearts. Are we ablaze with the fire of God's love, or have we allowed ourselves to become lukewarm and complacent?

The choice is ours to make, and it bears eternal significance. So may we be known as Christ's fervent and dedicated followers, shining with His light in a world desperate for the hope only He can bring.

Rekindled Love in These End Times

> *12 "And behold, I am coming quickly, and My reward is with Me, to give to every one according to his work. 13 I am the Alpha and the Omega, the Beginning and the End, the First and the Last." 14 Blessed are those who do His commandments, that they may have the right to the tree of life, and may enter through the gates into the city. 15 But outside are dogs and sorcerers and sexually immoral and murderers and idolaters, and whoever loves and practices a lie. Revelation 22:12-15:*

As we delve deeper into Jesus' words here, we discover His imminent return and its weighty consequences. He declares His swift arrival, bearing rewards for each person according to their works. Jesus establishes His divine authority as the Alpha and the Omega, the Beginning and the End, the First and the Last.

Blessed are those who faithfully adhere to His commandments, for they shall partake in the Tree of Life and enter through the city's gates. However, outside await the dogs, sorcerers, sexually immoral murderers, idolaters, and all those who embrace and perpetuate falsehood.

Jesus earnestly desires that we occupy ourselves with the tasks entrusted to us until His glorious return. He longs to reward us accordingly for our faithfulness and diligence.

Lukewarmness, on the other hand, is a slow but insidious killer. It mirrors the action of consuming a sugar-coated tablet of poison. With each layer of sugar that dissolves, the poison silently permeates the system, causing irreparable damage before one realizes the imminent danger.

In the spiritual realm, the context of being hot or cold revolves purely around our spiritual vitality. When people experience spiritual decline, they often remain oblivious to the gradual deterioration. Unlike the physical manifestation of hunger, spiritual decay remains inconspicuous until the realization dawns upon us one day, revealing the extent of our lukewarm state.

To combat lukewarmness, it is essential to be vigilant and heed the biblical principles that act as red flags. By engaging in spiritual disciplines, we can actively repel the encroaching killer.

Fervor, the antithesis of lukewarmness, entails acting with holy zeal, unwavering commitment, and promptitude guided by the Holy Spirit's peace, patience, and guidance. Recognizing the signs of lukewarmness in our spiritual lives empowers us to employ these spiritual disciplines, driving away complacency.

Lukewarmness emerges when our love for God fades and when our reverence for Him wanes. It manifests in claiming to be followers of Jesus while living self-sufficient lives, void of reliance on Him.

Lukewarm Christians may attend church, yet they remain content in their own ways, seldom applying the teachings they receive. Worship services become mere concerts, engaging only when the music aligns with personal preferences. Acts of charity are undertaken after calculating personal benefits.

In contrast, a Christian in a healthy relationship with the Lord performs good deeds out of a deep commitment and love for God. Lukewarm Christians dismiss their need for God, severing their connection to a vibrant relationship with Him, convinced of their self-sufficiency.

Let us be aware of the slippery slope that lukewarmness presents. May we kindle the flames of fervor within our hearts, drawing near to God and embracing His transformative power. Only then can we cast off the shackles of lukewarmness and live as vibrant, devoted followers of Christ, shining His light in a world longing for His truth and love.

Zero Commitment to Jesus

Can you recall the fervent passion that once ignited your heart in the early months after your rebirth in Christ? Jesus held an unrivaled position of importance in your life.

Sin lost its allure as you embraced God's true nature, and a resolute commitment to holiness defined your every thought and action. You viewed those who lived in sin, unaware of the call to a holy life, with zero tolerance.

Do you remember when you walked great distances to attend church, willingly sacrificing the money that could have been given to the tro-tro driver? It was a testament to your devotion, a silent dedication that went unnoticed by others. Those days of dawn broadcasts held immeasurable joy as you eagerly joined fellow believers in proclaiming the Gospel to your community.

I am confident that if given a chance, you could add countless more instances of your vibrant lifestyle and unwavering passion when Jesus found you, delivering you from sin and death, and forgiving all your past transgressions.

Yet, lukewarmness breeds a zero commitment to Jesus. I hope that such a description does not define you today.

No Witnessing

The lukewarm believer demonstrates a complete absence of witnessing and sharing their faith. They lack the zeal to evangelize and display apathy toward others. Even though they live amidst unsaved friends, siblings, colleagues, and loved ones, they make no effort to impart their faith.

They fail to fellowship with their neighbors, neglecting opportunities to discuss Jesus, God's love, and the imminent return of the Lord. Their focus remains solely on themselves, consumed by materialistic pursuits, deals, and transactions aimed at personal gain.

Take a moment to reflect on your own actions. When was the last time you boldly shared your faith and the love of God that resides within your heart? When did you last engage in a conversation about God's love? When did you last witness the transformative power of Jesus by rescuing someone from darkness?

Among the signs of a lukewarm believer, the most prominent is their self-centeredness. Their motivations, actions, and ambitions revolve entirely around themselves. As a result, they neglect the opportunity to impact and touch the lives of others, failing to leave a lasting legacy. History rarely treats them kindly because their lives are self-serving and lack genuine care for others.

Consider the words spoken in Judges 5:23:

"Curse Meroz," declared the angel of the Lord, "Curse its inhabitants bitterly, because they did not come to the help of the Lord, to the help of the Lord against the mighty."

This passage carries significant implications. It brings forth a double curse upon those who remain complacent in Zion, who display apathy and live solely for themselves, disregarding the work of the Lord. Everything we do in this life holds no eternal value or reward except that which is done for the Lord, His work, and His kingdom. These are the endeavors that carry eternal significance.

Let us strive to break free from lukewarmness, embracing a fervent love for God and a genuine concern for the salvation and well-being of others. By living a life that impacts and blesses those around us, we will leave a lasting legacy and find eternal fulfillment in the service of our Lord.

Rescue the Perishing

In the revelation received by the founder of the Salvation Army, he witnessed a sea filled with drowning believers. They were in desperate need of rescue, unable to save themselves. A rock and platform appeared, offering safety to those who could swim to it. However, while many found refuge on the platform and the rock, they remained indifferent to the plight of those still drowning.

Then, Jesus descended from heaven and entered the water to rescue the drowning people. He called out to those who were safe to join Him in the rescue mission, but they were content with their own comfort and began focusing on personal achievements and desires. Jesus continued to call for help, but nobody responded.

This dream symbolizes the call of Jesus for believers to actively participate in rescuing the perishing and caring for those who are dying spiritually. However, many are preoccupied with their own pursuits and survival and fail to respond to His call. They become self-centered and lose sight of the urgent need to save others.

In Luke 5, we encounter the story of Peter toiling all night without catching any fish. But when he obeyed Jesus and let down his net, he experienced a breakthrough. This story highlights the principle of seeking the kingdom of God and His righteousness first, with the assurance that all other things will be added unto us.

If we align ourselves with Jesus and partner with Him in rescuing the perishing, He will withhold nothing from us. He owns everything and has the power to provide, bless, increase, and multiply those who are committed to His ministry. The earth and its fullness belong to Him, and He is ready to work through us and bless us abundantly as we prioritize His mission.

Many people's struggle stems from their self-centeredness, where personal interests precede the Lord's work. But when our focus shifts to Him and His kingdom, God becomes obligated to provide, make a way, bless, and multiply us because of our unwavering commitment to His ministry.

Let us heed the call to rescue the perishing, share the love of God, and care for those dying spiritually. In doing so, we align ourselves with Jesus and open the door for His abundant blessings to flow into our lives.

Chapter 3

Beware of the End Time Lukewarmness

The lukewarm churchgoer makes no impact on the world and leaves no legacy, for their faith is inactive and their works are fruitless. A.W. Tozer

In the dimly lit prison cell, just before his martyrdom, the aged apostle, Paul, sat with parchment and quill in hand. Guided by the divine inspiration of the Holy Spirit, he penned a letter to his beloved protégé, Timothy.

With trembling urgency, he unveiled the signs that would mark the treacherous and turbulent days of the end times. His words carried a weight that transcended time and pierced the hearts of believers across generations. Today, as we stand on the precipice of the last days, Paul's message echoes with haunting relevance. This is what he wrote as a warning:

But know this, that in the last days perilous times will come: ² For men will be lovers of themselves, lovers of money, boasters, proud, blasphemers, disobedient to parents, unthankful, unholy, ³ unloving, unforgiving, slanderers, without self-control, brutal, despisers of good, ⁴ traitors, headstrong, haughty, lovers of pleasure rather than lovers of God, ⁵ having a form of Godliness but denying its power. And from such people turn away! ⁶ For of this sort are those who creep into households and make captives of gullible women loaded down with sins, led away by various lusts, ⁷ always learning and never able to come to the knowledge of the truth. ⁸ Now as Jannes and Jambres resisted Moses, so do these also resist the truth: men of corrupt minds, disapproved concerning the faith 2 Timothy 3:1-8

Once again, let us dive into the precise context of Paul's words and dispel any misconceptions. Contrary to some casual readers of the Word of God, Paul's message was not intended for unbelievers but held a profound directive for Timothy, who was entrusted with the weighty task of teaching and guiding the church. And even today, amidst the unfolding of the last days—the very culmination of the end times—these teachings retain their unwavering relevance.

When Paul speaks of "perilous times," he shines a light on the challenging and arduous periods believers may encounter. It is a solemn warning urging us to remain watchful and prevent these negative characteristics from infiltrating our lives.

The signs of lukewarmness that permeate our world serve as undeniable reminders of the times we inhabit. Therefore, we must venture deeper into the understanding of these signs, recognizing them as a resounding call to action—a summons to rekindle our fervor for God and ardently pursue His divine purposes with unwavering dedication.

Lovers of Self

Look around you and recognize the signs of these end times. The love of self is evident in the relentless pursuit of personal gain and recognition. But we have the power to break free from this self-centered mold. We have the opportunity to rise above the tide, reject the allure of selfish living, and walk in our Lord's footsteps.

Let us not be deceived by the trappings of this world, for they are fleeting and empty. Instead, let us fix our gaze upon the eternal, upon the things that truly matter. Let us cast off the chains of self-love and embrace a life of selflessness, compassion, and devotion to God and His kingdom.

Lovers of Money

In today's world, self and money reign supreme, driving societies with an unyielding force. A staggering revelation emerged in the wake of the pandemic: over five hundred new billionaires arose, their wealth soaring while others faced suffering and demise. The pursuit of money became a relentless quest, often at the expense of the masses.

How did this come to pass?

I cannot fathom the depths of its intricacies, but it is the reality we face. Money, the coveted prize, holds more sway than ever before. Godly virtues, character, and relationships have been relegated to the sidelines. It is money that takes center stage. Acquire it, amass it, regardless of the consequences or how it is obtained.

Countless individuals exist solely for money's sake. Their

entire lives are dictated and molded by its influence. Money has transformed into a deity, ruling over and controlling this generation.

People readily forsake their connection with God and anything and anyone for the sake of wealth. Money now determines behavior, shaping how individuals treat one another and their relationship with God and their fellow humans. It dictates their way of life, their choices, their decisions—every facet of their being.

With money in hand, one becomes celebrated and applauded. Attention and acceptance follow suit. Relevance and importance are bestowed upon those who possess what society desires.

It matters not the means employed to acquire it—whether through deceit, theft, or the breaking of rules—just acquire it. Thus, an insidious cycle ensues: individuals obtain money, elevate themselves as gods, and are esteemed highly by others. By any means necessary, they continue their pursuit of wealth.

Yet, it is vital to comprehend that money itself is not inherently evil. As long as we dwell in this mortal realm, money holds importance. It is the love of money, an insatiable craving, that breeds malevolence. This insatiable chase for wealth births all manner of trouble, and it is the very turmoil we witness unfolding before our eyes.

So, take heed, for the allure of money's power can corrupt even the noblest of hearts. Guard against its grip, maintaining a balanced perspective. Let not the love of money lead you astray, but instead, focus on the virtues of humility, generosity, and contentment.

Remember that true wealth lies not in the accumulation of

worldly possessions but in a heart attuned to love, the pursuit of righteousness, fulfilling the great commission, and serving the Lord.

Boasters

Boasting is another treacherous ground. To boast is to speak with excessive pride and to praise oneself extravagantly. It is a display of self-elevation that goes beyond simply acknowledging one's accomplishments or possessions.

When we achieve great things or accumulate wealth, there is no denying the facts. These accomplishments are tangible and undeniable. However, boasting arises when we speak too much about them, excessively elevate ourselves, and imply that our achievements are beyond the reach of others.

Let us reflect on the words of 2 Corinthians 10:12, 17-18, which caution against comparing and commending ourselves.

> *12 For we dare not class ourselves or compare ourselves with those who commend themselves. But they, measuring themselves by themselves, and comparing themselves among themselves, are not wise.*
>
> *17 But "he who glories, let him glory in the Lord." 18 For not he who commends himself is approved, but whom the Lord commends.*

We lack wisdom when we measure ourselves against our accomplishments or compare ourselves to others. True wisdom lies in glorying in the Lord, allowing our relationship with God to take precedence above all else.

It is intriguing that those who boast seldom speak of their relationship with God. Wise individuals recognize that their connection with the Holy Spirit surpasses worldly achievement or possession. They understand that it is not through self-praise that we are approved but rather through the commendation of the Lord.

In a world consumed by self-promotion, let us embrace humility and wisdom. Let us find contentment in our relationship with God, knowing that genuine approval comes not from the accolades of others but from divine commendation.

May we exalt the Lord above all else and let His glory shine through our lives. In doing so, we navigate the pitfalls of boasting, remaining grounded in the wisdom and grace bestowed upon us by our Heavenly Father.

I remember the excitement that filled my heart when I was born again. One of the greatest desires within me was to draw near to the spiritual fathers of our faith. It wasn't their earthly possessions, wealth, or the size of their ministries that captivated me. Instead, it was their deep spirituality, the tangible presence and anointing of God upon their lives, their profound understanding of the Holy Spirit, and the richness of their walk with God.

In their presence, I would eagerly seek their wisdom, asking spiritual questions pertaining to my journey of faith. There was an indescribable presence surrounding these men, something that went far beyond their external status. They possessed a spiritual magnetism, leaving me hungry for more of Jesus.

Take Dr. T.L. Osborn, for instance. He didn't have a megachurch or command a prominent spot on television. Yet, his impact on the world was immeasurable. In his company the presence of Almighty God was tangible, leaving an indelible impression on those who encountered him.

Similarly, men like Oral Roberts may not have been known for their impressive church buildings. Still, their faithfulness to their calling and unwavering commitment to their vision left a lasting legacy. Their lives radiated a unique and precious quality that compelled individuals to yearn for more of God and strive to emulate Jesus.

Sadly, today's landscape has shifted. The focus has shifted to numbers, material possessions, and personal achievements. The presence of God seems to have been overshadowed, and our priorities have become distorted.

I pray that God will graciously remind us again of what truly matters and help us realign our thinking and priorities. May we recapture the essence of genuine spirituality and pursue a deeper intimacy with our Heavenly Father, desiring His presence above all else.

As believers, our foremost priority upon waking each morning should be nurturing our relationship with God, for He is the ultimate source of our lives. Like David, we ought to confidently declare, *"The Lord is my light and my salvation; whom shall I fear? The Lord is the strength of my life; of whom shall I be afraid?"* Even when enemies and adversaries rise against us, they will stumble and fall in the presence of our mighty God.

However, in today's world, our priorities have been inverted. Money often takes precedence over God, family, and even our own well-being. It is crucial to understand that in God's divine plan, money is a tool—a vehicle entrusted to us to fulfill His purpose for our lives.

Its purpose extends far beyond paying bills, acquiring

possessions, or seeking personal pleasure. Silver and gold were created by God to serve His greater plan. Everything in our lives, including money, works together for our good when we love God and align ourselves with His purpose.

So, we must ask ourselves: Do we genuinely love God unconditionally, regardless of our circumstances? Are we willing to love Him like the three Hebrew young men who proclaimed, *"Our God is able to deliver us, and even if He chooses not to, we will not compromise our convictions and knowledge of God for acceptance, relevance, recognition, or attention?"* Their unwavering faith inspires us to remain steadfast in our devotion, even when faced with challenges or the allure of worldly gain. Let us emulate the heartbeat of Job.

Though he slay me, yet I will trust in him; but I will maintain mine own ways before him. He also shall be my salvation: for an hypocrite shall not come before him. Job 13:15-16

The Proud

In our present time, we encounter believers who exhibit unfortunate pride within their hearts. They carry themselves with haughtiness, harboring hurt and offense at every turn and finding fault in every situation.

Their interactions with others are tainted by their perceived status in society, their possessions, and their achievements. Regrettably, they display an absence of humility and compassion, looking down upon those they consider beneath them.

However, as followers of Christ, we are called to a different way of living. The Scriptures teach us the value of humility and the dangers of pride. It is through humility that we genuinely understand our reliance on God and recognize that everything we have and achieve is by His grace. Humility allows us to empathize with the struggles and shortcomings of others, extending compassion and understanding rather than disdain.

So let us walk humbly with our God, treating others with kindness and respect. May we cast aside the trappings of pride and embrace the virtue of humility, knowing that it is in humble service that we truly exemplify the character of Christ. In doing so, we will not only find favor with God but also create a positive and uplifting impact on those around us.

Blasphemers and Disobedience to Parents

The prevailing challenge of today's youth and children clearly indicates that we are indeed living in the end times. Disobedience to parents has become a significant issue, even within the Christian community. Naturally, there may not be a straightforward solution to this problem.

However, we must continue to fervently pray and trust in God's intervention, just as we witnessed in the parable of the prodigal son. Unfortunately, the younger generation is often swayed by their passions and heavily influenced by the internet and various forms of media on social platforms.

As parents, we must cultivate a strong and diligent parent-child relationship, allowing us to exert a positive influence that surpasses the impact of social media and external forces. While controlling social media may prove challenging, with the help of the Holy Spirit, we can guide our children toward healthy lifestyles and productive growth.

Reflecting on the journey of King Solomon, we observe his transformation in perspective over the course of his writings. In his early work, the Song of Solomon, he expressed a focus on passion, pleasure, and self.

However, as he matured, his subsequent book, Proverbs, revealed a shift in his understanding. Finally, in the later years of his life, as expressed in the Book of Ecclesiastes, he recognized the vanity of worldly pursuits and emphasized the paramount importance of fearing God and obeying His commandments.

Let us not wait until we reach the point of realizing the futility of our pursuits. Instead, let us embrace this truth now and strive to walk in alignment with God's will.

By prioritizing a reverent fear of God and obedience to His commandments, we can find true fulfillment and purpose in our lives. May this revelation guide our actions and help us lead the younger generation by example, instilling within them a love for God and a desire to live according to His divine principles.

Unthankful

In the tapestry of our existence, a troubling thread has woven its way into our lives – the thread of unthankfulness. We find ourselves living in a society where gratitude has become scarce, and the spirit of thankfulness has been overshadowed by a sense of entitlement and familiarity.

Gone are the days when expressions of gratitude were instilled in us from childhood when a simple "thank you" was the norm in response to acts of kindness or generosity. The art of appreciating the blessings bestowed upon us has been neglected, replaced by an unspoken expectation that others should meet our needs and desires without acknowledgment or appreciation.

Within families, this lack of gratitude has taken its toll. Children no longer utter words of thanks to their parents for their tireless efforts and sacrifices. Husbands and wives fail to recognize and express gratitude for the everyday gestures of love and provision. The sacred bonds of the family have been weakened by a lack of appreciation.

Familiarity breeds ingratitude as we become blind to the blessings that surround us. We take for granted the love, support, and provisions that others provide, failing to acknowledge the depth of their impact on our lives. Our memories have become short, forgetting the kindness shown to us in times past.

Yet, we must resist this tide of ungratefulness. Let us remember that gratitude is not a mere formality; it is a transformative attitude that shapes our character and enriches our relationships. Cultivating a heart of gratitude opens our eyes to the abundance of blessings bestowed upon us each day, both big and small.

Whether it is a heartfelt "thank you" to a loved one, an expression of gratitude to our heavenly Father, or a humble appreciation for life's simplest joys, let us reclaim the spirit of thankfulness. In an age where entitlement prevails, let gratitude be the counterforce that renews our hearts and restores our connections.

May we never grow familiar with the goodness of God and take for granted the love of those around us. Instead, may we embrace an attitude of gratitude, for it is in gratitude that we find joy, contentment, and the power to impact the lives of others. Let thankfulness guide our steps as we navigate the intricate tapestry of life.

Unforgiving

In the tapestry of relationships, there are those who harbor unforgiveness, unable to release the grip of past offenses. They cling tightly to the transgressions of others, never allowing forgiveness to take root. Instead, their tongues are quick to remind and recount the wrongs, weaving a narrative of resentment and bitterness.

Yet, in the depths of His mercy, Almighty God declares in Isaiah 43:25, *"I, even I, am He who blots out your transgressions for My own sake; and I will not remember your sins."*

If our God chooses to wipe away our sins and remember them no more, why do we persist in the remembrance of others' wrongs?

Jesus, in His infinite wisdom, urges us to embrace the path of forgiveness. He reminds us that if we withhold forgiveness from others, our Heavenly Father will likewise withhold forgiveness from us. The measure of forgiveness we extend reflects the measure of forgiveness we receive.

Consider the magnitude of forgiveness that Jesus teaches. When Peter questioned how many times he should forgive, Jesus responded, *"I do not say to you, up to seven times, but up to seventy times seven."* It is a call to an endless wellspring of forgiveness, unbounded by numerical markers or grudge-bearing.

Let us avoid falling into the trap of becoming perpetual record-keepers, tallying the offenses of others with meticulous precision. Instead, let our hearts be infused with the transformative power of forgiveness. It is a choice to release the weight of bitterness, relinquish the chains of unforgiveness, and walk in the freedom that forgiveness brings.

In our marriages and relationships, may we resist the temptation to constantly bring up past mistakes and transgressions. Instead, let us be spouses who nurture an environment of grace, compassion, and forgiveness.

For those who have suffered deep wounds and injustices, we can find comfort in the example of Nelson Mandela, who, after years of imprisonment, recognized that true freedom required leaving behind bitterness, unforgiveness, and offenses.

Unforgiveness should not be conditional, demanding that others earn our forgiveness or prove their repentance. True forgiveness transcends such barriers, extending grace without reservation. It does not mean turning a blind eye to wrongdoing but rather choosing to release the burden of resentment and seeking reconciliation when possible.

As believers, let us break free from the chains of unforgiveness and embrace the transformative power of forgiveness. By doing so, we create space for healing, restoration, and the boundless love of our Heavenly Father to flow through us.

May forgiveness be our anthem, woven into the fabric of our relationships, and may it set us free to live in the fullness of love, peace, and reconciliation.

Slanderers without Self-control

Within the spectrum of human emotions, anger holds a prominent place. From mild irritation to intense fury, anger can unleash a torrent of physiological and emotional changes within us. It is a natural response that evolved to help us confront threats and defend ourselves in the face of danger. However, when anger goes uncontrolled, it can become destructive, leading to harmful consequences for ourselves and those around us.

A bad temper often indicates difficulties in managing negative emotions and moods. While the term can vary in interpretation, ranging from occasional irritability to more severe anger disorders, it signifies a struggle to maintain composure and respond to provocations in a healthy and balanced manner. Individuals lacking self-control may resort to destructive behaviors, damaging property, and engaging in vicious verbal attacks.

Yet, as believers, we are called to a higher standard. Self-control is a fruit of the Spirit, a mark of spiritual maturity and growth. It is the ability to master our reactions and responses, to rule our spirits rather than be governed by our emotions. In the book of Proverbs 16:32, it is proclaimed that *"he who is slow to anger is better than the mighty, and he who rules his spirit than he who takes a city."*

When left unchecked, a bad temper can have far-reaching consequences, affecting not only our mental and physical health but also straining relationships with others. Even without engaging in violence or explosive outbursts, a volatile temper can create an environment of tension and unease, hindering the development of healthy and supportive connections.

Recognizing the importance of self-control and its role in fostering harmonious relationships, it becomes imperative to cultivate the fruit of the Spirit.

Therefore, let us strive to embrace self-control, knowing that our ability to govern our own hearts is a testament to the work of the Holy Spirit within us. By taming our tempers, we create an atmosphere of peace, understanding, and love, nurturing healthy relationships and fostering personal growth.

Brutal Despisers of Good

Another troubling phenomenon exists in our times – the celebration of evil and the disdain for all that is good. Those who embrace this mindset have become brutal in their outlook, forsaking the virtues that once held significance in society. Instead, they enjoy indulging in darkness while disregarding the call to pursue righteousness and honor.

What was once considered noble and praiseworthy is now met with scorn and contempt. Goodness is mocked, and those who embody it are belittled and marginalized. In pursuing personal pleasure and self-gratification, these individuals prioritize their desires above their devotion to God.

The Scriptures teach us to love the Lord our God with all our strength and might and to give Him the highest priority in our lives.

However, this commandment holds little weight for those who embrace this brutal mindset. Their allegiance lies with whatever brings them immediate gratification, be it the allure of a nightclub or the pursuit of worldly pleasures. They offer justifications and excuses for their absence from prayer meetings and worship services, their hearts focused solely on themselves.

Yet, we are called to a higher standard. We are called to be a light amid the darkness, to stand firmly for what is good and righteous. The path of pleasure-seeking and the celebration of evil leads only to emptiness and spiritual bankruptcy. It is an illusion that blinds us from the true joy and fulfillment that comes from a life dedicated to God's purpose.

Having a Form of Godliness but Denying its Power

Another sign of the times is individuals who bear the appearance of godliness yet deny its true power. These individuals possess the knowledge and language of believers, effortlessly mimicking their words and actions. They appear devout on the surface, but their hearts remain untouched by the transformative power of a genuine encounter with God.

Their understanding of faith is purely superficial, lacking the experiential depth of a genuine relationship with the Holy Spirit. They may engage in religious practices, speak in tongues, and perform rituals, but their faith lacks substance. Their actions are driven by a desire to fit in, to project an image of piety rather than a sincere devotion to God.

The Scriptures warn us to turn away from such individuals, recognizing that their empty forms of godliness can lead us astray.

Therefore, it is crucial for believers who find themselves entangled in this deceptive façade to seek help immediately. They must humbly acknowledge their need for true spiritual transformation and seek guidance from those who can lead them to a genuine encounter with God.

True godliness is not a mere outward show but a transformation of the heart and a surrender to the power of God. It is an ongoing journey of growth and intimacy with the Holy Spirit, where the presence of God becomes evident in our lives through His power at work within us.

Let us guard ourselves against the allure of empty religiosity and seek to cultivate a genuine relationship with God. May our faith be rooted in a personal encounter with Him, where His power can transform us from within and manifest in our words, actions, and character.

May we continually seek the guidance of mature believers who can help us navigate the challenges of faith and lead us closer to the true power of godliness.

Chapter 4

Don't Die a Slow Spiritual Death

Lukewarm Christians are those who want to comfortably benefit from the kingdom of Christ without passionately following the King Himself. - David Platt

A sinister culprit exists, leading to a slow demise of the spirit—the decline of your spiritual fervor. But what does it truly mean to experience this fervor? It transcends mere words, for it is a profound and sacred connection, an upward surge of the soul in response to God's ever-reaching presence. Each day, His arms stretch wide, a gentle beckoning that invites you into His embrace.

"Come unto Me" resonates through the ancient scriptures, a divine chorus of calls that resound with unwavering love. In explicit declarations and subtle whispers, God unveils His heart, yearning for our presence within His sacred chambers, where deep communion awaits.

Yet, how do you fare on the scale of spiritual disciplines? It is through this lens that the pulse of your spiritual vitality can be measured, revealing whether you dance with life or languish in the grip of slow spiritual decay and retrogression.

How is the gold become dim! How is the most fine gold changed! Lamentations 4:1

Spiritual Discipline 1 – Praise and Worship

> *"Woman," Jesus replied, "believe me, a time is coming when you will worship the Father neither on this mountain nor in Jerusalem. You Samaritans worship what you do not know; we worship what we do know, for salvation is from the Jews. 23 Yet a time is coming and has now come when the true worshipers will worship the Father in the Spirit and in truth, for they are the kind of worshipers the Father seeks. God is spirit, and his worshipers must worship in the Spirit and in truth."* John 4:21-24

At the core of our spiritual journey lies the essence of worship—a heartfelt recognition and honor bestowed upon God. It is an act that transcends self-centeredness, redirecting our gaze to Jesus and kindling within us a fervent adoration. Worship emerges as our primary response to the eternal nature of God and the wondrous works He has bestowed upon us.

God, in all His majesty, deserves our praise, worship, and adoration. He merits the highest honor within our hearts, reigning supreme over every facet of our existence. A heart filled with awe, gratitude, and deep appreciation becomes a sanctuary of worship.

True worship begins by acknowledging in the depths of our being the majestic nature of God and revering Him for who He truly is. It emanates from our unique personhood and individuality, intertwining with our knowledge of God's attributes. We cannot revere someone whose qualities we do not comprehend.

As we delve into an intimate understanding of God's character, we naturally extend honor and reverence within our hearts. This knowledge shapes the words we speak and the actions we display during church services, becoming a tangible expression of our worship—an art that reveals the profound connection between our hearts and the One who holds the highest place within them.

Characteristics of the True Worshipper

Intimate Knowledge of God: True worshippers have a personal and deep relationship with the Father. They know and embrace their identity as children of God, fulfilling the promise in John 1:12.

Active Relationship: They cultivate an active and ongoing relationship with the Father, Son, and Holy Spirit. They nurture their connection with the divine through daily engagement with God's Word (Joshua 1:8; Psalm 1:1-4).

Solitude with God: True worshippers set aside dedicated time to be alone with the Father. In these sacred moments, they humbly acknowledge and affirm the revelations they have received from the Father, fostering a deeper understanding of His character.

Obedience: They walk in daily obedience to the Father's will. Understanding that true discipleship is marked by obedience, they actively align their lives with the teachings of God's Word.

Revelation of God: True worshippers possess a revelation of the Father that extends beyond mere knowledge. Like Paul, they fervently pray for others to experience a profound revelation of God. They encounter the Father in the midst of life's circumstances, growing in their understanding of His ways

Surrendered Hearts: The Father reigns as the supreme authority in the lives of true worshippers. They willingly yield their hearts to His rule, placing Him in the highest position of honor and priority.

Daily Experience of God's Power: True worshippers actively seek to witness God's power at work in their lives. In a world shrouded in darkness, they eagerly anticipate opportunities to testify and say, "God has done it again," as they witness His miraculous interventions.

Gratitude and Thanksgiving: They cultivate a habit of counting their blessings and expressing gratitude to the Father. Daily, they approach Him with a heart overflowing with thanksgiving, recounting His goodness and the manifold blessings He has bestowed upon them.

Praise & Thanksgiving

Within praise and thanksgiving lies a profound truth that transcends mere words. It is the acknowledgment of someone's deeds and the heartfelt gratitude that flows from those deeds. For true praise to exist, there must be an undeniable impact, a tangible expression of goodness.

We cannot offer genuine thanks to someone who has done

nothing for us or for those we don't know. In the context of God's infinite works, we find the wellspring of our praise and thanksgiving, for He continues to reveal His power and grace in our lives.

But let us not be deceived, for the mere phrase "I praise you" uttered during a church service does not encompass the depth of genuine praise. It is not a superficial utterance mandated by a "praise and worship" session.

On the contrary, genuine praise requires something more significant—it demands that God occupy first place in our hearts. It beckons us to seek His perspective in every situation, to understand His expectations and to align our actions to please Him amidst our circumstances. It is a sincere questioning that arises from a heart that truly places God as its foremost priority.

Worship, likewise, is not confined to the act of singing biblical songs or showcasing musical talents.

It transcends outward demonstrations and resides in the depths of our spirits. It is the embodiment of a surrendered soul, yielding to God in absolute submission. It is the manifestation of a human spirit that exalts God, placing Him firmly on the throne of our hearts.

Beware, for the spirit of worship can wane, slowly giving way to lukewarmness, until it finally grows cold. Never take God's goodness for granted, nor miss an opportunity to bow before Him.

Instead, let your spirit be stirred to honor Him spontaneously, for that is the essence of true worship—a sacred surrender that ignites the fire of adoration and reverence.

Spiritual Discipline 2 – Embracing Solitude and Silence

Amid life's ceaseless clamor, a sacred practice holds the key to hearing the gentle whisper of God's voice—solitude and silence.

In these moments of intentional seclusion, away from the distractions that besiege us, we find ourselves attuned to the divine presence. As the psalmist wisely imparts, "Be still and know that I am God" (Psalm 46:10).

For us, as followers of Christ and especially as leaders in the Christian faith, it is crucial that we not only hear the voice of God but also respond with unwavering obedience.

Jesus expects nothing less from His devoted disciples—to listen attentively and follow His divine guidance. In the midst of our bustling lives, where noise and commotion threaten to drown out the still, small voice, we must cultivate an intimate familiarity with God's gentle whispers.

Consider, in the sanctuary of your personal communion with God, where do you place your phone? Is it faithfully by your side, ready to divert your attention with every incoming call or message? What could possibly be so pressing that it cannot wait until you have completed your precious moments of solitude and silence before Almighty God?

Therefore, let us not engage in frivolous games regarding matters of profound significance.

Beware of compromising these invaluable periods of solitude and silence before God, for they clearly indicate your trajectory towards lukewarmness. Guard these moments fiercely, for it is within the quiet sanctuary of your soul that you encounter the divine, where transformative encounters await.

May we not succumb to the allure of the urgent but prioritize the eternal, immersing ourselves in the sacred stillness that draws us closer to the heart of God.

Spiritual Discipline 3 – The Art of Journaling

Within the pages of a journal lies a treasure trove—a testament to our thoughts, emotions, experiences, and heartfelt prayers. It is through the practice of journaling that we weave a tangible tapestry of our relationship with God.

In this fast-paced world, where the cacophony of life threatens to drown out the whispers of the Holy Spirit, journaling serves as an anchor, a written testimony of our encounters with God.

As we pour out our hearts onto the pages, we find solace in the act of releasing the swirling thoughts that occupy our minds. Journaling becomes a gateway to redirect our focus from ourselves and fix our gaze upon our relationship with God. It becomes a sacred dialogue, a space where our experiences, both in the solitude of our closets and amidst the mundane tasks of life, find their voice.

Yet, the benefits extend beyond the present moment. A written record becomes a precious repository, a tangible reminder of God's unwavering faithfulness in our lives. It serves as a compass, guiding our future steps as we revisit the footprints of the past.

With each journal entry, we are nudged towards growth, and prompted to reflect upon our spiritual journey. We refuse to remain stagnant, for the written testimony invites us to embrace the transformative power of God in our lives.

Spiritual Discipline 4 –Studying God's Word

To grow spiritually, mere glances at the pages of the Bible will not suffice. It is through the diligent study of God's Word we unearth its hidden treasures and allow its transformative power to permeate our lives. This is not a casual encounter but a purposeful journey that demands our full attention.

> *And Jesus answering said unto them, Do ye not therefore err, because ye know not the scriptures, neither the power of God?*
> Mark 12:24

Beyond the surface-level reading at the break of dawn, we are called to delve deeper. Armed with the tools of exploration —concordance, study Bibles, and other invaluable resources— we embark on a quest to unravel the intricate tapestry of divine wisdom.

We tread the paths of analysis, connecting the threads of scripture and drawing insights from their harmonious resonance. We are not satisfied with superficial understanding; instead, we yearn for profound comprehension.

In the pursuit of studying God's Word, we cultivate a hunger for its timeless truths, eagerly immersing ourselves in its sacred passages. We embrace the discipline of memorization, etching verses upon our hearts, embedding them in the very fabric of our being.

We refuse to let this passion wane, for we recognize that within the depths of scripture lies a wellspring of revelation, an ever-flowing stream that nourishes our souls.

Spiritual Discipline 5 – Meditation

Meditation is a profound practice that transcends the boundaries of mere study. It is an invitation to immerse ourselves in a single concept, often a verse from the Scriptures. As we engage in this contemplative journey, we open ourselves to the whispers of God, beckoning Him to speak to us through and about the chosen idea.

Drawing inspiration from the apostle Paul's exhortation, we fix our thoughts on what is true, noble, right, pure, lovely, admirable—allowing our minds to dwell on the splendor of these virtues (Philippians 4:8).

Through meditation, we unveil deeper layers of God's character and unearth profound truths that surpass the boundaries of conventional exegesis.

A seemingly simple concept, such as holiness or joy, becomes a gateway to a profound encounter with God. In meditation, we surrender ourselves to the teaching of the Holy Spirit, allowing Him to illuminate our hearts with revelations that extend beyond the analytical realm of study.

Here, in this rich tapestry of devotion, we find a longstanding tradition within the Christian Church—a tradition that beckons us to explore the depths of our faith through contemplation.

While meditation and study often intertwine, they possess distinct experiences. Studying the Word of God equips us with a framework, offering analytical insights that fuel our meditative endeavors. It is through the study of God's Word that our minds undergo a transformation, aligning with the transformative power of divine truths (Romans 12:2).

As we delve into the Scriptures, faith blossoms within us, for faith comes by hearing the message, and the message is heard through the living Word of Christ (Romans 10:17).

While meditation is a practice that bridges the analytical and devotional realms. Through the synergy of meditation and study, we embark on a transformative journey where our minds are renewed, and our faith is fortified.

Spiritual Discipline 6 - Prayer

Prayer stands at the heart of the vast spiritual disciplines, radiating life and transformation. It is the gateway to intimate communion with the Father, a sacred connection that breathes vitality into our existence. True prayer is more than mere words; it is a divine symphony that creates and reshapes life itself.

Imagine prayer as the very breath that sustains the Christian life, infusing it with divine essence and purpose. Without prayer, we become mere walking shells, disconnected from the vibrant life—the Zoe life—that God offers us. We are reduced to creatures rather than co-heirs, devoid of the fullness of our identity as children of God.

Yet, when we pray, we step into a profound reality. We enter a sacred space where the supernatural intersects with the natural, where heaven's power is unleashed upon the earth. Through prayer, we align our hearts with God's will, inviting His transformative work into our lives and the world around us.

Prayer is not a passive endeavor but an active participation in the divine story. It is the means through which we express our deepest longings, confess our shortcomings, intercede for others, and seek guidance and wisdom.

In the embrace of prayer, we find solace, strength, and supernatural encounters that transcend the limitations of our human existence. At the place of prayer, we superimpose and execute His Will, and His Kingdom mandate is made manifest.

Spiritual Discipline 7 - Fasting

In the realm of spiritual disciplines, there is a profound practice that transcends mere self-denial—it is fasting. Some may define fasting as abstaining from anything that obstructs our communion with God; indeed, many things can hinder our connection with the Holy Spirit.

However, according to rich biblical teachings, fasting specifically entails abstaining from food.

Fasting is more than a physical act of refraining from nourishment; it is a spiritual discipline that stirs the depths of our being. By willingly embracing self-denial in the realm of food, we open ourselves to a journey of heightened awareness and spiritual awakening. It is a deliberate choice to prioritize our hunger for God above our physical appetite.

Fasting is not a solitary pursuit but is intricately intertwined with prayer. While fasting and prayer are distinct disciplines of spiritual exercises for spiritual encounters, they intertwine like threads in a tapestry, weaving a transformative experience.

Through fasting, we demonstrate our earnestness and desire to seek God's face, draw closer to Him, and align our will with His divine purpose.

Fasting provides a unique space for spiritual refinement and discernment. As we relinquish physical nourishment, we awaken our spiritual senses to hear God's voice more clearly, to perceive His guidance, and to deepen our intimacy with Him.

It is an invitation to surrender our earthly desires and allow God to work within us, purifying our motives, strengthening our faith, and empowering us to overcome spiritual obstacles.

While it is essential to consider any medical conditions that may prevent fasting from food, we encourage you, whenever possible, to embark on this transformative journey.

Let your fast be a tangible expression of your hunger for God, a demonstration of your willingness to lay aside earthly comforts for the sake of spiritual growth.

Spiritual Discipline 8 – Celebration and Communion

In the ancient setting of the Passover, on the eve of His sacrificial death, Jesus instituted a profound fellowship meal that continues to resonate through the ages.

It is a sacred observance, a symbolic feast that encapsulates the essence of Christian worship—a dynamic interplay of remembrance, present reality, and future hope.

Within the confines of this commemorative meal, we partake in an "acted-out sermon," where our Lord's life, death, and resurrection are vividly remembered.

We behold the cross and the empty tomb, acknowledging the depths of His love and the victory over sin and death. Yet, it is not a mere backward glance but a forward gaze that fuels our hearts.

We anticipate the glorious return of Christ when His

kingdom shall be fully revealed, and all things will be made new.

Lukewarmness finds its foothold when we neglect these spiritual disciplines. It is not a matter of cherry-picking some while ignoring others.

Each spiritual discipline, collectively, contributes to the development and sustenance of our spiritual fervor. They intertwine, synergistically igniting our spiritual temperature and aligning us consistently with the heart of God and His Holy Spirit.

The Scriptures assure us that those who wait upon the Lord will find their strength renewed. They will soar on wings like eagles, walk and run without growing faint or weary.

Yet, waiting on the Lord becomes a distant memory in the realm of lukewarmness. Impatience pervades our hearts, and we succumb to the allure of instant gratification. Ours has become a microwave generation, craving immediacy and lacking the patience to seek God in unhurried communion.

Evaluating Your Spiritual Temperature

Take a moment to engage in a simple exercise, a self-assessment, to gauge your spiritual temperature. With sincerity and introspection, you can discern whether you find yourself growing cold, burning hot, or residing in the unsettling space of lukewarmness.

Ultimately, you are the best judge of your spiritual state at any given moment. My role here is to assist you in fostering and maintaining a perpetual spiritual fervor.

On a scale of 1 to 7, with 7 representing the highest and 1

the lowest, evaluate where you currently stand on this faith journey, using the template provided on the following page.

Consider taking this test periodically, every three months, to discern whether you are progressing, regressing, or remaining stagnant in your spiritual journey.

Remember, this is not a test to earn points or impress others —it is a deeply personal and sincere reflection of your relationship with God. Approach it with honesty and humility, seeking divine guidance and assistance as you navigate the path of spiritual growth.

May your sincerity open the door for a transformative encounter with the Holy Spirit.

Consciousness of Your New Identity							
I am certain that I am a child of God	7	6	5	4	3	2	1
My life always reflects that I am born-again	7	6	5	4	3	2	1
My hatred for sin is on the increase	7	6	5	4	3	2	1
Knowledge of who God is:							
Increased Faith in God	7	6	5	4	3	2	1
Acknowledging God as Wise always	7	6	5	4	3	2	1
Choosing God's word above all others	7	6	5	4	3	2	1
Letting God have His way in your life	7	6	5	4	3	2	1
Perception of God is always solid	7	6	5	4	3	2	1
Hunger for Direction from God:							
Searching God's word: Study of the word	7	6	5	4	3	2	1
Desiring to hear the Voice of God	7	6	5	4	3	2	1
Desire to dwell in God's presence daily	7	6	5	4	3	2	1
Prayer is the number one priority for me	7	6	5	4	3	2	1
Fasting is something I do often	7	6	5	4	3	2	1
Conscious of God's ways than opinions	7	6	5	4	3	2	1
Led by the Spirit							
Knowing right from wrong instantly	7	6	5	4	3	2	1
Informed by the Holy Spirit daily	7	6	5	4	3	2	1
Doing right by the Holy Spirit	7	6	5	4	3	2	1
My spiritual gifts are active	7	6	5	4	3	2	1
A life of honoring God							
Praising and worshipping God all the time	7	6	5	4	3	2	1
Thanking God throughout my days	7	6	5	4	3	2	1
I write testimonies of God's goodness	7	6	5	4	3	2	1
I share my testimonies all the time	7	6	5	4	3	2	1

Chapter 5

The Necessity of Christian Fellowship

"Fellowship isn't simply friendship. It's friendship with a purpose: to serve God together, to support each other in our common mission, to build one another up." - Rick Warren

If your journey in Christianity has covered considerable ground, I would assert that you don't find kinship with those who declare that Christianity is a solitary discourse between the individual and their God, without any necessity for fellowship with other believers.

Such a perspective is not just divergent, but it borders on heresy in relation to certain scriptures that underscore the personal rapport between you and God.

The journey of faith, as we've previously explored, possesses a powerful vertical dimension that connects us directly with God. But, it's equally imperative to recognize that Christianity also entails a significant horizontal facet. The author of the Book of Hebrews elucidates this point precisely:

¹⁹ Therefore, brethren, having boldness to enter the Holiest by the blood of Jesus, by a new and living way which He consecrated for us, through the veil, that is, His flesh, ²¹ and having a High Priest over the house of God, ²² let us draw near with a true heart in full assurance of faith, having our hearts sprinkled from an evil conscience and our bodies washed with pure water. ²³ Let us hold fast the confession of our hope without wavering, for He who promised is faithful. ²⁴ And let us consider one another in order to stir up love and good works, ²⁵ not forsaking the assembling of ourselves together, as is the manner of some, but exhorting one another, and so much the more as you see the Day approaching. Hebrews 10:19-25

This passage adeptly encapsulates both the vertical and horizontal dimensions of the Christian experience. It underscores the significance of both aspects, even reproaching those who distance themselves from the collective assembly of believers.

The Sustaining Power of the Bread of Life

In my earlier days of faith in Christ, a period nestled comfortably in the annals of yesteryears, attending church and returning home fulfilled and gratified was not just a habitual practice but an intrinsic norm.

A routine, if you may, that found us yearning for Sunday's dawn. Even now, after the final notes of the Sunday service worship have faded, I find myself wrestling with the mundane notion of lunch. An activity as rudimentary as eating suddenly appears tedious and prosaic against the spiritual satiation received from the church.

Indeed, the silence that ensues post-service seems to reverberate with echoes of divine words, resonating in the caverns of my heart and mind. This invisible symphony engulfs me, making it difficult to focus on the ritual of consuming food.

Only a meal of exceptional quality, a feast that matches the grandeur of the spiritual banquet I've partaken in, can lure me towards the dining table. Such is the depth of satisfaction I attain from church, akin to a banquet for the soul that leaves me satiated to the core.

Church for the Lukewarm

For the lukewarm Christian, attending church services seems to have lost its allure. Once a bustling hub of spiritual connection, the church now feels akin to a desolate desert, bereft of the nourishing waters of fear, love, hunger, and passion for God.

This lukewarm mentality, akin to tepid water that neither quenches thirst nor soothes the soul, manifests itself in an obstinate refusal to participate in the ministry of the church, a practice expected and cherished by the Lord Himself.

The notion of serving in God's house, once a beacon drawing them towards meaningful service for God, now seems shrouded in an inexplicable haze of apathy. Once held with fervor and enthusiasm, commitment to any aspect of God's work appears to dissipate like mist under the harsh glare of indifference.

Despite the church opening its arms wide, offering ample opportunities for service and fellowship, lukewarm Christians perceive this embrace as hollow, barren, and devoid of the vibrancy and warmth that once drew them in.

These Christians need cajoling, coaxing, and almost pleading to engage; their participation is contingent on persuasive arguments and calculated reasoning. As if the fulfillment of spiritual duty were a debate to be won or a transaction to be negotiated.

They yearn for compelling arguments like "10 reasons why you should attend church regularly" or "10 reasons to engage in evangelistic outreach," disregarding the simple fact that their duty to God and fellow believers should be reason enough.

Typically, their presence graces the church only on Sundays, their faces missing from church-related activities sprinkled throughout the rest of the week. Their excuses are plenty and varied, each one a testament to their spiritual detachment. They resist staking a claim in any specific part of the church, preferring instead to hover on the periphery, removed from the central pulse of the congregation.

In their minds, they exist as a class apart—the nobility of Christianity. They believe they've ascended to a higher realm, maintaining a societal standard that prohibits them from fraternizing with regular home cell attendees or members of church departments. In their skewed perception, these active members are merely struggling souls, lesser beings in the grand scheme of a spiritual hierarchy.

Their only tangible contribution lies in the ritualistic act of offering tithes and offerings on Sundays, a mechanistic practice devoid of the fervor that once imbued it. Their spiritual journey seems to be more about maintaining appearances than seeking true communion with God, which calls for deep introspection and awakening.

The Bible proclaims that he who walks in the light and abides in it enjoys fellowship with the brethren. If we are truly walking in the light, we will exhibit humility, grace, compassion, and recognize the needs of others, and enjoy their fellowship.

Jesus blessed those who thirst and hunger for righteousness, promising they shall be filled. Where is this thirst and hunger in today's church? We show up on Sunday mornings, and that is all until the following Sunday. Oh, that God might stir and rekindle our fervor, reviving us once more!

The Nobles of Tekoa

Nehemiah 3:5 brings to life an intriguing scenario, *"Next to them the Tekoites made repairs; but their nobles did not put their shoulders to the work of their Lord."* This seemingly straightforward text encases a rich tapestry of human behavior and class dynamics that demands exploration and understanding.

Let's travel back to the era of ancient Tekoa, a small town south of Bethlehem. This region, known for its rugged terrain, was populated by hardy people renowned for their resilience and hard work. It was also home to the prophet Amos, a humble shepherd who became a powerful voice for godly justice despite his lowly status.

The spirit of community work was strong among the ordinary Tekoites, as demonstrated in rebuilding Jerusalem's walls under Nehemiah's guidance. But the nobles, the so-called crème de la crème of society, remained conspicuously absent from this collective endeavor.

The Snare of Indifference

The nobles, ensconced in their societal pedestals, saw themselves as the titans of their era. Picture them as the influencers of the ancient world, their voices reaching far corners of the Earth, their influence palpable in both local and foreign circles.

They were like the luminaries of our modern world—wealthy entrepreneurs, celebrities, and politicians—whose lives are often characterized by their detachment from the plight of ordinary folks. Encased by their aura of supremacy, they erected invisible walls, making themselves unapproachable and defiant to any call for communal participation.

A story from contemporary times may further illuminate this. Let's consider the tale of a successful businessman, Mr. Robinson, who was a prominent local church member.

Mr. Robinson was known for his immense wealth but not so much for participating in church activities. His interaction with the congregation was minimal, often limited to brief appearances on Sundays.

However, when a financial crisis hit Mr. Robinson, his detached facade began to crumble. He turned to the church community for support, a community he had largely ignored during his days of prosperity.

It was during these trying times that he came to appreciate the true essence of wealth, not as a means for personal aggrandizement but as a tool to serve a larger purpose, a sentiment echoed in the Biblical verse, *"For it is easier for a camel to go through the eye of a needle than for a rich man to enter the kingdom of God"* (Luke 18:25).

Like Mr. Robinson, the nobles often hold back from investing their resources and talents into the church. They cloak their reluctance under the guise of carefully crafted excuses, alluding to why they can't employ their talents for the benefit of the church.

This unwillingness reflects an inherent self-obsession that overshadows other vital aspects of life, such as spirituality, community, and charity. Imagine the transformative impact if these individuals channeled their influence, skills, and resources into the church and other community projects.

This reflection is not an indictment but a gentle reminder and plea to you. It urges you to avoid slipping into spiritual lukewarmness, a state where faith is reduced to a mere accessory in one's life.

Let this historical account and contemporary tale serve as your guiding beacon, helping you steer clear from the dangerous rocks of complacency and self-centeredness. Let them inspire you to fulfill your divine responsibilities with grace and humility.

Chapter 6

Pleasing People: A Hidden Trap for Believers

Woe unto you, when all men shall speak well of you! For so did their fathers to the false prophets. Luke 6:26

Living in the world, we rely heavily on our senses. Unfortunately, these senses often focus on what's right in front of us and can cause us to place our faith on the back burner.

While we believe in God, we can easily get swept up in life based on what we can see, hear, and touch. This can lead us to worry more about making others happy, even if it means we're not focusing on making God happy.

We must remember that being warm or cold, as Jesus mentioned in the book of Revelation, isn't about how we interact with others. Instead, it's about how strong our connection with God is, which should guide how we live our life on earth.

In this chapter, we will explore some attitudes and behaviors that may seem fine on the surface but can actually douse our spiritual enthusiasm.

These are signs that someone's love for God might be cooling down, shifting from a passionate flame to a lukewarm simmer or even a cold indifference. By understanding these hidden traps, we can avoid them and keep our spiritual fire alive.

Being Ashamed of Christ and Our Spiritual Leadership

Jesus said in Luke 9:26:

> *For whosoever shall be ashamed of me and my words, of him shall the Son of man be ashamed, when he shall come in his own glory, and in his Father's, and of the holy angels.*

The Apostle Paul also wrote to his son Timothy:

> *Be not thou therefore ashamed of the testimony of our Lord, nor of me his prisoner: but be thou partaker of the afflictions of the gospel according to the power of God 2 Timothy 1:8*

The spiritual trailblazers who journeyed before us held no trace of embarrassment or shame about their faith in God and Christ. What's more? God, too, expressed no hesitance in being known as their God. This profound truth resonates in the teachings of Paul, Peter, and the author of the Book of Hebrews, who all touched upon this topic:

¹⁶ For I am not ashamed of the gospel of Christ, for it is the power of God to salvation for everyone who believes, for the Jew first and also for the Greek. Romans 1:16

¹⁵ But let none of you suffer as a murderer, a thief, an evildoer, or as a [g]busybody in other people's matters. ¹⁶ Yet if anyone suffers as a Christian, let him not be ashamed, but let him glorify God in this matter. ¹⁷ For the time has come for judgment to begin at the house of God; and if it begins with us first, what will be the end of those who do not obey the gospel of God? 1 Peter 4:15-16

¹⁵ And truly if they had called to mind that country from which they had come out, they would have had opportunity to return. ¹⁶ But now they desire a better, that is, a heavenly country. Therefore God is not ashamed to be called their God, for He has prepared a city for them. Hebrews 11:15-16

In stark contrast to the saints of the early church who braved societal scorn with unwavering faith, the modern believer appears to be entangled in the snares of social perception. This dynamic is evident when individuals shy away from openly acknowledging their faith in Christ, afraid of how this religious identity may be received.

Consider a scenario where a Christian businessman negotiates a lucrative deal with a non-believer. How many such individuals readily assert their faith amidst non-Christian colleagues? How many stand their ground, refusing a proposition that may potentially tarnish their Christian persona?

Regrettably, many succumb to silence, prioritizing financial gain over the proclamation of their Christian values. Once this compromise is made, it sets a pattern. Gradually, the Christian businessman's actions bear little reflection of his faith or the teachings of the Bible.

Suppose you're at a restaurant. Would you offer a prayer before partaking in your meal, just as you would during a church gathering where food is served? Or does the fear of being identified as a believer dissuade you?

These instances may seem insignificant, trivial even, in the grand scheme of our spiritual journey. However, these seemingly minor omissions accumulate and grow, causing a gradual shift in our spiritual orientation. Before you know it, offering a simple prayer to acknowledge God becomes a matter of internal debate.

Jesus warned that if we deny Him before others, He will deny us before His Heavenly Father. The full implications of this admonishment are shrouded in mystery, making it all the more prudent to avoid finding ourselves in such a predicament.

Thus, displaying shame or embarrassment towards Christ and our faith indicates a lukewarmness seeping into our spiritual lives. It directly impacts our identity as children of God. It's akin to renouncing our spiritual heritage simply because it might cost us worldly gains or our reputation among peers.

Some will even go as far as joining in criticizing the church just to gain acceptance from their peers. This, we must remember, is a path riddled with spiritual perils.

> *Blessed is the man that walketh not in the counsel of the ungodly, nor standeth in the way of sinners, Nor sitteth in the*

seat of the scornful. But his delight is in the law of the LORD; And in his law doth he meditate day and night. And he shall be like a tree planted by the rivers of water, That bringeth forth his fruit in his season; his leaf also shall not wither; And whatsoever he doeth shall prosper. Psalms 1:1-3

Afraid of Man but No Fear of God

In a world that often puts human perspectives above God's truth, there's a growing push towards a mindset and lifestyle that is distinctly human-centered.

This trend spans various spheres of life, from academia, where you're expected to cite the 'original' author of a statement to avoid charges of plagiarism, to the realm of religion, where those chosen as God's instruments often garner more attention than God Himself. This shift of focus, of allegiance, is palpable.

Even the church isn't immune to this issue. We find ourselves gravitating towards pleasing people rather than God. Consider, for example, the matter of tithing.

When a senior pastor announced his intention to scrutinize tithe records, congregation members were quick to 'settle' outstanding tithes, an obligation they had previously neglected. Herein lies the irony: they seemed to fear the pastor, a man, more than God, who initially asked them to give their tithes.

Could it be that our inability to physically see God is subtly translating into a perception that He's distant or that His words carry less weight compared to those of our fellow humans?

If you find yourself growing increasingly concerned about societal opinion rather than focusing on God's directives, it could be a symptom of spiritual lukewarmness.

It suggests that your allegiance is wavering, shifting from God toward the world. For many compelling reasons, it's essential to remember that it's always better to align ourselves with God than with mortal beings. After all, God's faithfulness, unlike human fidelity, is unwavering and everlasting.

Upholding Philosophers and Ideologists above God

In the case of intellectual discourse and academia, who do we often look to for authority and insight? For many, the go-to references are renowned philosophers like Plato or Socrates or thought leaders like Benjamin Franklin rather than Jesus or biblical figures like Moses or Isaiah.

It's often deemed more sophisticated to quote an academic scholar than to quote Jesus, even though many scholarly assertions are paraphrases or interpretations of biblical teachings. Curiously enough, despite their roots in scripture, these insights often go unacknowledged as such.

The reality is that within scholarly work, Jesus is rarely directly cited. He is not seen as a scholar; instead, interpretations of His teachings by others are referenced. This disconnect from the original source means that if the interpretation is flawed, the subsequent understandings will also be flawed.

It's clear that the world of academia is primarily built on human perspectives rather than God's truth. Sometimes these align, given that biblical teachings have universal applications, but without acknowledging God as the source, the depth of understanding is lost.

Noticing a tendency to lean more towards worldly philosophers and ideologists rather than the Word of God is a warning sign. It signals a potential shift towards spiritual lukewarmness. God's Word may not seem as fervent or impactful as when you first encountered it.

Suppose you find yourself swayed more by the predictions of scientists, futurists, financial moguls, or billionaires than by the deep convictions of the Holy Spirit. In that case, your spiritual fire may be dimming, propelling you toward a state of lukewarmness.

The Apostle Paul encapsulates this concern eloquently in his letter to the Romans (Romans 1:18-23). He cautions about the danger of suppressing divine truths and replacing the glory of God with human-centric beliefs and constructs.

> *[18] For the wrath of God is revealed from heaven against all ungodliness and unrighteousness of men, who suppress the truth in unrighteousness, [19] because what may be known of God is manifest in them, for God has shown it to them. [20] For since the creation of the world His invisible attributes are clearly seen, being understood by the things that are made, even His eternal power and Godhead, so that they are without excuse, [21] because, although they knew God, they did not glorify Him as God, nor were thankful, but became futile in their thoughts, and their foolish hearts were darkened. [22] Professing to be wise, they became fools, [23] and changed the glory of the incorruptible God into an image made like corruptible man—and birds and four-footed animals and creeping things. Romans 1:18-23*

Similarly, Christians striving for recognition in scholarly circles may find themselves torn. Some might even compromise their understanding of God's Word to fit into worldly academic paradigms.

This conflict isn't likely to subside until the end of days, and as believers, we need to be steadfast and intentional in upholding God's truth above worldly wisdom.

Paul also warns us in 1 Corinthians 3:18-21 that the wisdom of this world is foolishness in God's sight.

> *[18] Let no one deceive himself. If anyone among you seems to be wise in this age, let him become a fool that he may become wise. [19] For the wisdom of this world is foolishness with God. For it is written, "He catches the wise in their own craftiness"; [20] and again, "The Lord knows the thoughts of the wise, that they are futile." [21] Therefore let no one boast in men. For all things are yours.* 1 Corinthians 3:18-21

Human wisdom will never surpass divine wisdom. If you find yourself excessively entangled in worldly wisdom, to the point where it clouds your biblical understanding of reality, it's time to reflect.

Such a shift indicates a possible drift into lukewarmness, a dilution of your passion for God's truth, and a misplaced allegiance to the world's celebrated thinkers.

Faith in Yourself Rather than God

Have you ever encountered individuals attributing their accomplishments solely to their hard work and determination?

Yes, there's no denying the importance of diligence, akin to the relentless industriousness of the ant. However, our prosperity is not solely a result of our toil and sweat.

It's crucial to remember that God empowers us to acquire wealth, and it's not apt to forget Him as our primary source. A gradual reliance on self can dangerously displace God from the central position He should occupy in our lives. Living independently without God's guidance and presence in our life is a perilous path.

A fervent Christian whose faith is ablaze never misses an opportunity to proclaim God's goodness. In fact, they often go out of their way to initiate conversations about God, not necessarily limited to praise and worship services. They don't reserve acknowledging God's greatness only for special occasions.

If you notice a pattern in your conversations where you continuously tout yourself as the sole architect and the driving force behind your success, neglecting to credit God's grace, it's a warning sign. You may be subtly shifting from a passionate follower of Christ to a lukewarm believer.

The world's motivational speakers frequently advocate for self-belief and mind power as the keys to achievement. Similarly, proponents of positive thinking echo these sentiments.

However, these ideologies often lack the crucial context of faith in God, the divine orchestrator who facilitates all our accomplishments, even the ones that initially seem impossible. Often, these perspectives marginalize God, promoting self-reliance over dependence on God.

Believing in one's abilities and maintaining a positive outlook are essential traits, but they should not replace our faith in God. If the emphasis on self-belief begins to overshadow your faith in God, you are at risk of becoming spiritually lukewarm.

It's essential to keep our faith firmly rooted in God, acknowledging Him as the ultimate source of all our accomplishments.

Expecting God to Conform to Our Ideas

Sometimes, we encounter individuals who seem to believe that God should adhere to human notions rather than the other way around.

Those expressing such perspectives may believe that God should have acted differently in certain situations. They construct scenarios and expectations that God should comply with, and when He doesn't, they draw far-reaching conclusions about His nature.

But can your faith in God truly remain fervent if you expect Him to align with your perspectives or those of the majority? It's undeniable that no human ideas or collective thought can surpass the wisdom and profundity of God's plans and ways. Some paths appear correct to an individual but can ultimately lead to a downfall.

> *There is a way which seemeth right unto a man, but the end thereof are the ways of death. him.* Proverbs 14:12

> *Be not wise in thine own eyes; fear the LORD, and depart from evil.* Proverbs 3:7

Indeed, the pace of human advancement in the 21st century is staggering. The era of artificial intelligence is upon us.

For instance, we now have wristbands that monitor our heart rate and physiological activities, offering guidance on our behaviors, such as reminding us to stand and stretch if we've been sitting too long.

While such innovations can benefit our health, it would be a mistake to surrender our lives entirely to artificial intelligence, particularly given the acknowledged potential risks associated with this technology.

The reality is that no level of human progress can dictate God's ways. After all, where does our wisdom and ability to create such technologies come from, if not God, who breathed His Spirit into us, making us living souls?

If your conversations are dominated by technology and its increasing influence on our lives, it indicates a shift away from God's original design. Technology can never replace God, nor can its offerings substitute for God's eternal promises.

In essence, it's vital to maintain a balanced perspective. While we can appreciate and harness the benefits of technological advancements, they should never overshadow our reliance on and reverence for God. Otherwise, we risk drifting into a state of spiritual lukewarmness, where the warmth of our faith in God is gradually replaced by the cold logic of machines.

Refusing to Honor God

Disregarding the honor due to God could manifest in different ways, one of which is taking our very existence for granted. If you find yourself awakening each morning without acknowledging that it's purely by God's grace that you're alive, it may indicate a slow spiritual deterioration.

Perhaps your biology teacher didn't emphasize that without God's Spirit continually breathing life into us, our bodily cells, tissues, and organs wouldn't possess the vitality needed to perform the essential functions defined in science books as characteristics of living things, such as moving, excreting, growing, and breathing.

The laissez-faire attitude encapsulated by "whatever will be will be" severely disrespects God. Yet, since this phrase was popularized by a philosopher, many people base their entire lives on it, ignoring the vibrant existence that depends on God and His purpose for our lives.

Similarly, when God brings blessings our way throughout the day, some fail to offer even a simple word of gratitude, recognizing Him as the source.

Is there any shame in using the phrase "God is wonderful in His creation" instead of attributing marvels to "Mother Nature"?

Nature didn't create itself; God brought it into existence with all its intricate details. So why does humanity struggle to honor God for His marvelous works?

Humanity seems to employ every terminology possible, excluding mentioning God as the One responsible for all the good we witness around us. This indifference aligns with an age-old pattern of warfare where efforts, led by Satan through men, are being made to erase anything that refers to or honors God. This concept is encapsulated in Psalm 2:

"Why do the nations rage, And the people plot a vain thing? The kings of the earth set themselves, And the rulers take counsel together, Against the LORD and against His Anointed, saying, 'Let us break Their bonds in pieces and cast away Their cords from us.'"

Here, the Psalmist points out that God's laws and principles for life on earth have been viewed as shackles that need to be cast off. All the individuals described in this passage are not honoring God. They lack a fervor for God; their spiritual condition is cold. It is perilous for a follower of Christ to fall into such a mindset.

As believers, we must be vigilant against the subtle presentations by the world's wise that gradually pull us away from God's principles. A life that fails to honor God is a life on the path toward lukewarmness.

Live To Please the Lord

We as believers must center our hearts, minds, and lives on pleasing God rather than men. In an increasingly human-centered world, prioritizing God's commands, principles, and will seems countercultural and daunting.

Yet, in this lies the true essence of our faith. God's validation and approval should always triumph over human applause.

As we navigate through the varying demands of life, let's continually remind ourselves that our spiritual relationship with God far outweighs earthly acceptance.

Let's strive to remain steadfast, keeping our spiritual fire alive rather than drifting into lukewarmness due to societal pressure. For it is in pleasing God that we find our true identity, purpose, and joy. May our lives consistently reflect our reverence and devotion to Him as we diligently work to ensure that our love for God never wanes but always burns bright.

> *When a man's ways please the LORD, he maketh even his enemies to be at peace with him.* Proverbs 16:7

Chapter 7

Why that Appetite for Worldliness?

Worldliness proposes objectives which demand no radical breach with man's fallen nature; it judges the importance of things by the present and material results; it weighs success by numbers; it covets human esteem and wants no unpopularity; it knows no truth for which it is worth suffering; it declines to be a 'fool for Christ's sake'. - Iain Murray

The city was buzzing with life and energy as if it held a secret that all of its inhabitants were seeking. Skyscrapers kissed the skyline, a testament to mankind's triumph and ambition. In every corner, one could find the lustrous material allure of the world, tempting even the most stoic souls.

But amidst this whirl of glamour and power, a quiet question lingers - why do we crave this worldliness? Why is it that we are often swayed by the glitter of gold, the lust of the flesh, and the pride of life? Why does this worldly appetite persist, even when we know these worldly things are fleeting?

Let's delve into these challenging questions and dissect this seemingly insatiable hunger for worldliness that plagues so many, obscuring the light of God's love. We begin with the words of the Apostle John:

> *15 Do not love the world or the things in the world. If anyone loves the world, the love of the Father is not in him. 16 For all that is in the world—the lust of the flesh, the lust of the eyes, and the pride of life—is not of the Father but is of the world. 17 And the world is passing away, and the lust of it; but he who does the will of God abides forever.* 1 John 2:15-17

Decoding Worldliness

To navigate our earthly journey effectively, it's essential to comprehend some foundational truths.

First, we are spiritual beings experiencing a mortal existence. Numerous amenities, which we often take for granted, are indispensable to our lives on Earth. It would be preposterous to deny their necessity.

Eating, clothing ourselves, enjoying various forms of entertainment, and working to earn a living for our basic needs - all of these and many more are prerequisites for our transitional lives in this world.

When we interpret the concept of worldliness from the Biblical viewpoint, we are not denouncing these necessities as inherently evil. What we need to recognize is that while we live in physical bodies, our true essence is spiritual.

Any undue emphasis on the physical body at the expense of our spiritual needs tends to introduce discord into our earthly lives. This imbalance forms the basis of the Biblical admonitions against worldliness.

The Bible defines worldliness as the disproportionate pursuit of these physical needs, which eventually hampers our spiritual and moral growth. Worldliness signifies an imbalanced lifestyle that excessively prioritizes materialistic needs over spiritual well-being.

When the Bible states that eating and drinking are worldly, it doesn't advocate for starvation. Instead, it cautions against overindulgence, gluttony, and the excessive chase of other materialistic needs required for life on Earth.

The caution is not against the essentials themselves but against allowing these essentials to dominate and dictate our lives, thereby clouding our spiritual clarity.

Chasing Trends Vs. Pursuing Devotion

In the rapidly advancing world of technology, the term 'trending' has become a buzzword. It's what people are urged to pay attention to and to follow diligently.

Unfortunately, many seem to place a higher premium on keeping abreast of what's trending than spending time in morning devotions to discern God's guidance for the day. In other words, people are chasing trends more fervently than cultivating their faith.

One may argue that their faith is built on these trends - they become the primary focus of conversation, day after day. This obsession with trends is why panic sets in when the trends start looking unfavorable.

Worldly happenings have gradually become our focal points. Now, don't misconstrue my words. I am not advocating complete ignorance of our surroundings. Instead, I am urging a reassessment of priorities. If we are honest with ourselves, most trending issues have little bearing on our journey toward a meaningful life with Christ.

Many trends revolve around entertainers and athletes whose lives have become so public that even mundane events in their lives become news. When these celebrities experience everyday events like pregnancy or breakups, it becomes a trending topic. These individuals have evolved into influencers, especially for the younger generation. However, their influence often extends no further than their fame, popularity, and wealth.

Countless people are spending an inordinate amount of time on social media, sharing one joke after another, often sharing content that can be spiritually and morally harmful. This behavior gives the impression of time squandering.

Social media platforms are inundated with content promoting immorality in one form or another. People patronize these platforms for various reasons, rarely considering how they could better utilize this time to build a solid future for themselves. Social media has become the norm, and anyone who isn't on it is viewed as old-fashioned.

We should never foster a passion for fleeting trends over a passion for God, His words, and His deeds. Instead, we must refocus our interests, prioritizing spiritual growth and divine guidance over chasing temporary trends. The allure of the trend may seem enticing, but the enduring satisfaction comes from pursuing a life of devotion.

One story that illuminates this point is about a young man named Peter who had just graduated from college. Energetic, smart, and full of potential, he was ready to take on the world. He had grown up in a good Christian family and was deeply rooted in his faith. Yet, like many young adults, he was also excited about exploring new experiences and embracing the vibrant, tech-savvy world around him.

Not long after starting his first job, Peter found himself caught up in the whirlwind of the modern corporate world. His colleagues were all active on social media platforms, following the latest trends and often discussing the daily happenings of celebrities.

Wanting to fit in and be part of the conversation, Peter started dedicating a substantial portion of his time and energy to keeping up with these trends.

As he dove deeper into this world of trends, he noticed changes in himself. His morning devotions became shorter, eventually becoming sporadic and then nonexistent.

He found himself increasingly obsessed with what was "trending" and began mimicking the lifestyle of celebrities. As a result, he started feeling an unusual restlessness within himself, a nagging sense of emptiness that he had never experienced before.

One day, while scrolling through his social media feed, he came across a post from an old friend from his church group, a simple Bible verse, *"For what will it profit a man if he gains the whole world, and loses his own soul?"* (Mark 8:36).

It was as if a jolt of electricity went through him. He realized he had been losing himself while trying to keep up with the world's trends.

Peter decided to make a change. He rekindled his relationship with God and began spending time each morning in prayer, reading the Bible, and getting actively involved in church again.

While he didn't completely disconnect from social media, Peter became more discerning about how much time and energy he spent on it. He began to realize the importance of balancing his attention between the physical and spiritual aspects of his life.

He also discovered that his influence could be used for good. Instead of just sharing trends, he started sharing verses, positive messages, and his own personal stories of faith on social media. Peter found that this not only enriched his spiritual life but also influenced others positively.

This story is a powerful reminder that while trends are a part of our world, they shouldn't overshadow our pursuit of a meaningful, faith-filled life. Instead, we should use our platforms, whether in person or online, to spread positivity and share the love of God. After all, trends may come and go, but the Word of God stands forever.

Living According to the Flesh

To gain a deep understanding of worldliness, we must first discern its definition as given by the Word of God. Worldliness, as described in the Bible, involves the lust of the flesh, which represents a yearning for sensual satisfaction.

In addition, it includes the lust of the eyes, symbolizing an excessive desire for the finer things in life, and the pride of life, epitomizing self-satisfaction in who we are, what we possess, and what we have achieved.

The Apostle John aptly outlines these characteristics of worldliness, interestingly, his description mirrors the events that led to Adam and Eve's disobedience in the Garden of Eden.

Genesis 3:6-7 recounts:

"So when the woman saw that the tree was good for food, that it was pleasant to the eyes, and a tree desirable to make one wise, she took of its fruit and ate. She also gave to her husband with her, and he ate. Then the eyes of both of them were opened, and they knew that they were naked; and they sewed fig leaves together and made themselves coverings."

Eve was drawn to what was pleasing to her eye and appealing to her palate. So, she chose the tempting fruit over obedience to the Creator, thereby marking the inception of mankind's love and worship of created things rather than the Creator himself.

The allure of worldly things often targets our most basic, untamed desires and human inclinations. As Jesus stated, merely casting a lustful gaze upon a woman amounts to committing adultery. If unchecked, our eyes and other senses can lead us down paths we should not tread, enslaved by our unbridled desires and longings.

As followers of Christ, we are summoned to imitate Christ by resisting the allure of worldly pleasures. While this does not suggest that we should shun the blessings and joys that God has provided (Ecclesiastes 3:13; 5:19; 1 Timothy 6:17), it does mean that we should indulge within the parameters defined by our loving heavenly Father. Our utmost devotion and passion should be reserved for God alone.

While we may physically inhabit this world, we must not allow it to shape our identity and principles; we are not of this world. Our life's standards should not reflect those of the world but align with God and His Word. The world will try to tempt us with the very gifts intended for our good, leading us astray when we succumb to such lures.

Isn't it curious that the Bible acknowledges that "money answers all things," yet it also warns us that "the love of money is the root of all evil"?

This seemingly paradoxical statement emphasizes the importance of balance. The compulsive desire to accumulate wealth beyond what we genuinely require is classified as covetousness in the Bible.

Simultaneously, the Bible recognizes that God endows us with the power to generate wealth. It is essential, then, to maintain equilibrium—securing our legitimate needs without succumbing to the pursuit of money for its own sake.

There exists a timeless hymn, the refrain of which is often sung with heartfelt passion:

> *"Turn your eyes upon Jesus,*
> *Look full in His wonderful face,*
> *And the things of the world will grow strangely dim,*
> *In the light of His glory and grace."*

As the lyrics suggest, the more your gaze is fixed on Jesus, the more the allure of worldly things diminishes. To truly understand the struggle between the Spirit-directed life and worldly temptations of the flesh, it's essential to categorize the "things of the world" into two broad categories.

The first category consists of certain lifestyles and behaviors diametrically opposed to spiritual growth. They bind you to a life led by the flesh, constantly seeking to fulfill the whims of your undisciplined, baser instincts.

The Bible warns us of the incessant conflict between the flesh and the spirit, claiming that the two are fundamentally incompatible. Therefore, if one is entrenched in the desires of the flesh, one drifts further from the life in Christ.

The second category includes elements necessary for our well-being but has been exalted to the status of a god, causing us to become their slaves. Be it the inordinate love for material possessions, the obsession with social status, or the relentless pursuit of physical gratification, these can become distractions that divert us from our spiritual path.

Whether outright indulgence in destructive behaviors or overemphasizing worldly possessions, both scenarios pose significant challenges to our spiritual journey. Thus, the lyrics of the hymn serve as a potent reminder to keep our focus on Jesus, for in the radiant light of His glory and grace, worldly distractions recede into the shadows.

Chapter 8

Watch These Killer Attitudes

Spiritual stagnation is a result of spiritual negligence. - T.D. Jakes

In the darkness, they lie in wait, stealthy and cunning, patiently biding their time. They aren't tangible threats, like a wild beast or an oncoming storm. Instead, they are more insidious, more elusive, and yet, far more dangerous. They are attitudes — the hidden killers lurking in the shadows of our hearts.

In this chapter, we dive into the murky waters of our inner attitudes that often mask themselves in the garb of societal norms or personal convenience. Their power lies in their subtlety; our mission is to unmask and expose them to the light.

Complacency

Let us tune in to the echo of the Church's complacency in Revelation 3:17-20, a complacency that resounds so clearly in our modern circumstances.

> *17 Because you say, 'I am rich, have become wealthy, and have need of nothing'—and do not know that you are wretched, miserable, poor, blind, and naked—*
> *18 I counsel you to buy from Me gold refined in the fire, that you may be rich; and white garments, that you may be clothed, that the shame of your nakedness may not be revealed; and anoint your eyes with eye salve, that you may see.*

The Church declares, 'I am rich.' Indeed, the Church today brags of wealth beyond measure, of pockets that run deep, of the ability to possess whatever their heart desires.

The Church today revels in abundance, in a life of plenty, and in wealth that has multiplied beyond its wildest dreams. It boasts of independence, of being self-made, with no need for anything or anyone.

The Church today proclaims, 'I am self-sufficient.' It dismisses the need to reach out to others, to lend a hand, to offer comfort. It basks in its own glory, cocooned in a palace built from wealth and power.

But let us pause to hear the response from God: 'As God, I am omniscient. I see the beginning from the end. I know who you truly are. Your self-perception may be a skewed image filled with wealth and prosperity, but that is not how I see you. Your self-view starkly contrasts the true image I see and hold as your Creator.

God retorts, 'You think you are rich and self-sufficient? Let me reveal your true state. You are miserable and wretched, trying desperately to fill the emptiness within you. The void that neither money nor pleasures of life can fill, the void that can only be filled by Me.'

There lies a stark contrast between how the Church perceives itself and how God perceives the Church. And undoubtedly, God's perception carries more weight. With His words, God challenges the Church's complacency, a complacency that is all too common in our world today.

God further accuses the Church of being blind and naked. The Church, veiled in an illusion of prosperity, is blind to its own state of vulnerability.

God extends an offer to the Church – an invitation to seek riches from Him, the gold tried by fire. He offers the white garments to cover the Church's nakedness and shame, and the eye salve to enlighten the Church to the revelation. This offer is born from His love for the Church and His desire to see it zealous and repentant.

The Church today is in danger of falling into the same complacency as the Church in the Book of Revelation. We measure success by wealth and numbers, losing sight of the essence of who we are – our identity as children of God. What defines us is not our possessions but our relationship with God, our humility before Him.

We must guard against complacency born from wealth and abundance. If we let our guard down, these material possessions may blind us to our spiritual needs.

The Snare of Indifference

Recently, I was asked about the extent of my ministry – the number of members and branches I had around the globe. My response was, I didn't know. Why would that be of relevance? Is that the metric used to gauge our relationship? Who I am is not determined by figures, wealth, buildings, or worldly possessions.

My essence is revealed in my moments of humility when I am on my knees before God. So, I implore you, don't define me by my material assets or attire. Remember what Jesus taught: a man's life does not consist of the abundance of things he possesses. This calls for vigilant caution, lest wealth and abundance breed complacency within us. They certainly will if we permit it.

Take, for instance, a story from the 1950s. A seasoned preacher had been ministering at a church for several weeks when a vibrant young evangelist arrived. Blessed with a powerful gift, this evangelist sparked a revival within the church. Attendance soared, and the congregation's spirits were uplifted.

However, the older preacher was troubled by a sight he'd witnessed the day before the evangelist's first sermon: the younger man had been seen entering a place considered unbecoming for a follower of Christ.

Simultaneously, there was a longstanding parishioner in the church, an elderly woman who had walked the path of righteousness for over sixty years. The older preacher wondered why God had chosen the young evangelist to bless the church instead of her, leading him to consult God on this matter.

The Lord explained that the young evangelist, unfamiliar with the city, had unwittingly walked into a questionable establishment but immediately exited upon realizing his mistake. By the time the older preacher passed by, the young man was already outside, leading him to pass judgment based on a partial view of events.

Meanwhile, the elderly lady, seemingly a paragon of virtue and piety who'd been born again for over sixty years, had lived in silent rebellion against God for over forty years. Her impeccable image was misleading.

Complacency, in a spiritual context, is a grave sin. So often, we focus on physical transgressions, but there are significant spiritual sins as well — arrogance, criticism of others, unforgiveness, taking offense, and withholding what rightfully belongs to the Lord and His house.

Those who step into the church with the mindset that they are beyond reproach, unmoved by any sermon or minister, should guard against a hardened heart and a life in rebellion against Jehovah Adonai.

According to the Scriptures, absolute perfection is an aspiration we strive for but can only fully attain when the rapture occurs. Thus, regardless of how virtuous or righteous you consider yourself today, there may still be issues God is addressing in your life, perhaps even unbeknownst to you. Therefore, I implore you to relinquish any trace of complacency.

Complaining and Grumbling

The following attitudes I want to address are a silent but deadly pair: complaining and its close kin, grumbling. These traits often manifest in individuals who relentlessly criticize leadership and seemingly find fault in nearly everything leadership undertakes.

Let's be clear, leaders are human, and being human, they make mistakes. Yet, due to their prominent positions, their errors tend to be amplified compared to the mistakes of those standing in the shadows of the congregation. God has instructed us to fervently pray for those in positions of authority. Instead of grumbling about your pastor, fervently pray for him. Rest assured that God knows how to correct His children should they stray from the path of obedience.

Those who perpetually complain and grumble usually contribute minimally to the growth and development of the church. Here's an important observation: those individuals who are actively engaged, always available, and wholeheartedly invested in the church's work tend to have the leader's ear.

They don't resort to slander or backbiting to grab the pastor's attention. Instead, their dedicated, faithful engagement in the work of the church and their knack for getting things done naturally draw the pastor's attention.

Often, they don't even approach the pastor directly. Instead, more often than not, it's the pastor who seeks out their opinions regarding the church's operations. And guess what? The pastor listens to them because they have demonstrated an unwavering commitment to the church's mission.

When individuals nurture a spirit of complaint, there seem to be no bounds. They complain about their parents, church leaders, political figures, essentially everyone and everything.

This constant murmuring, grumbling, and ceaseless discontent can quickly become a defining trait. God does not look kindly upon a spirit entrenched in complaining and grumbling.

One compelling incident that underscores God's distaste for

complaining and grumbling can be found in the annals of the Israelites' exodus through the wilderness. The whole story, recorded in Numbers 12:1-10, is a testament to this divine dissatisfaction:

> *Then Miriam and Aaron spoke against Moses because of the Ethiopian woman whom he had married; for he had married an Ethiopian woman. ^{2} So they said, "Has the Lord indeed spoken only through Moses? Has He not spoken through us also?" And the Lord heard it. ^{3} (Now the man Moses was very humble, more than all men who were on the face of the earth.) ^{4} Suddenly the Lord said to Moses, Aaron, and Miriam, "Come out, you three, to the tabernacle of meeting!" So the three came out. ^{5} Then the Lord came down in the pillar of cloud and stood in the door of the tabernacle, and called Aaron and Miriam. And they both went forward. ^{6} Then He said,*
>
> *"Hear now My words: If there is a prophet among you, I, the Lord, make Myself known to him in a vision; I speak to him in a dream. ^{7} Not so with My servant Moses; He is faithful in all My house. ^{8} I speak with him face to face, Even plainly, and not in dark sayings; And he sees the form of the Lord. Why then were you not afraid To speak against My servant Moses?" ^{9} So the anger of the Lord was aroused against them, and He departed. ^{10} And when the cloud departed from above the tabernacle, suddenly Miriam became leprous, as white as snow. Then Aaron turned toward Miriam, and there she was, a leper.*

The striking part of this narrative is that Moses, the very man they criticized, interceded on their behalf, pleading, "God, please heal her." Yet, Miriam was required to spend seven days outside the camp in her leprous state. This was God's profound way of expressing His contempt for complaining and grumbling, particularly against His chosen leader.

The Apostle Paul, reflecting on these historical events, offers a cautionary message to the church in Corinth about the dangers of complaining and grumbling, recognizing it as an attitude that displeases God. He writes in 1 Corinthians 10:8-11:

> *⁸ Nor let us commit sexual immorality, as some of them did, and in one day twenty-three thousand fell; ⁹ nor let us tempt Christ, as some of them also tempted, and were destroyed by serpents; ¹⁰ nor complain, as some of them also complained, and were destroyed by the destroyer. ¹¹ Now all these things happened to them as examples, and they were written for our admonition, upon whom the ends of the ages have come.*

Through this, Paul reinforces the notion that the mistakes and trials of the Israelites were recorded as lessons for future believers, warning against behaviors such as grumbling and complaining that lead to destruction and discord, thereby reminding them to remain mindful of their conduct.

Easily Offended

Another treacherous attitude that can seep into the fabric of our faith is the propensity to be easily offended. Some individuals, susceptible to the slightest wind of disagreement or difference, wrap themselves in their emotions like a cloak, becoming hypersensitive to the point where any minor remark or differing opinion triggers offense.

A pastor's sermon intended for the entire congregation is misconstrued as a personal attack. A minor disagreement with a into a personal affront.

Though offended, the tragedy is that such individuals continue to partake in church activities, subtly spreading their bitter attitude like a contagion. Their grievances are numerous, born out of interactions with various individuals in the congregation. There's hardly anyone they've engaged with who hasn't offended them in one way or another.

Living like a time bomb, they sit in anticipation of the slightest trigger to explode into anger. Occasionally, they find themselves at odds with someone, unable to pinpoint the root cause of their frustration, yet certain of the discord between them.

People in their company walk on eggshells, forced to monitor every word and action meticulously to avoid offense. When people are overly cautious in your presence, they cannot express their true selves.

Instead, they provide you with the superficial facade that you desire, and once they step out of your sphere, they revert to their true selves. The corrosive impact of such sensitivity not only saps individual relationships but also undermines the communal harmony that is so central to the life of the church.

If you identify with any of the following traits, it may be time to seek assistance, as these characteristics often define those who are easily offended:

Imposing Their Values on Others: Such individuals are prone to projecting their values, beliefs, and insecurities onto others, often mistaking their personal convictions for the truth.

Tendency Towards Anxiety: People prone to anxiety may feel an intense need to control their environment. When their perceived truths are challenged, they tend to become defensive and irritable, portraying an image of being easily offended.

Inner Suffering: Being overly sensitive and easily offended can often be a cover for personal pain and suffering. Isolation and social withdrawal may be their unique coping mechanisms.

Issues with Insecure Attachment: From a developmental perspective, they may feel a constant undercurrent of danger or uncertainty. They might struggle to express their needs healthily and instead blame others and play the victim.

Insecurity: These individuals often seek validation from others rather than practicing self-love and acceptance. Being easily offended gives them a sense of control and enables them to manipulate others through guilt.

Self-centeredness and Egotism: Easily offended individuals can be obstinately self-involved, shutting down rational discourse by taking offense and solidifying their beliefs as facts.

Craving for Attention: Those who are easily offended may be craving attention. Complaining and expressing offense provides them an avenue to command the attention of others, enabling them to recite their grievances, which validates their perceived victimhood.

As we bring this chapter to a close, it's time to take a moment of introspection. If you identify with any of the attitudes explored here - complacency, complaining and grumbling, or being easily offended - it's crucial to confront these truths head-on.

Being sincere with oneself can be a difficult task. It demands a high degree of honesty and vulnerability. But remember, acknowledging a problem is the first step toward addressing it.

Should you find these attitudes lurking within you, don't despair. Recognize that these traits are not an indelible part of your character but behaviors that can be unlearned. Asking for help is not a sign of weakness; on the contrary, it's a testament to your strength and determination to bring about change in your life.

First of all, seek God's help. Then speak to mature friends in the church, church leaders, or pastors who can provide perspective and guidance. Their wisdom, compassion, and insight can prove invaluable as you navigate your journey with Christ.

Also, remember to harness the power of prayer. Turning to God offers peace and strength in times of self-doubt or struggle. You're not alone in this journey - you have the Holy Spirit always ready to provide comfort and direction. So, start today, and look forward to a brighter, healthier, and more satisfying tomorrow with Christ at the center of your life.

Chapter 9

Walk in the Zeal of the Lord

Let not your zeal flame out in one act, but let it be the perpetual motion of your life. – Thomas Adams

Fire. It crackles and snaps; it lights up the darkness and chases away the chill. It's both mesmerizing and powerful, capable of warmth and destruction.

Now, imagine that fire within you, within your spirit. That's zeal – it's your spiritual fire, your burning passion for the Lord.

It's a powerful force that should never be allowed to dim, for once extinguished, it leaves one in a state of spiritual lukewarmness, a state far removed from the divine radiance of faith.

In this chapter, we are embarking on an essential journey. Together, we'll explore how to fan the flames, ensuring your spiritual fire burns perpetually. This is not just about religious adherence but a passionate, intimate relationship with the Lord.

So, buckle up, dear reader, because we're about to dive into the profound depths of walking in the zeal of the Lord. Then, let this chapter guide you through the practical ways of keeping that fire alive and vibrant within you.

We will let the numerous accounts in the Bible of those whose zeal for the Lord burned brightly inspire us to embrace the same fervor in our own faith journeys.

Phinehas

Phinehas' demonstration of zeal is not just a remarkable episode but a significant turning point in the biblical narrative. It illustrates how one man's passionate commitment to God's righteousness can drastically alter the course of events.

In Numbers 25, the Israelites were camped in Shittim and began to indulge in sexual immorality with Moabite women, a clear violation of God's laws. Moreover, these women invited them to participate in the sacrificial feasts to their gods, leading the Israelites astray into idolatry. As a result, God's anger burned against Israel, and a devastating plague struck the people.

Amid this calamity, an Israelite man openly brought a Midianite woman into his tent in the sight of Moses and the whole congregation. It was a brazen act of defiance against God's commandments.

Phinehas, a priest, and Aaron's grandson, witnessed this blatant disregard for God's law. Consumed with zeal for the Lord's honor, he took a spear, followed the Israelite into the tent, and killed both the Israelite man and the Midianite woman. This decisive action halted the plague ravaging the people of Israel.

Phinehas' act was not born out of personal vengeance or

hate but out of a profound respect for God's holiness and a fervent desire to uphold God's law among His people. His zeal reflected a deep understanding of the severe implications of disobedience against God's commandments, and he was not afraid to stand up for God's honor, even when it meant going against the tide.

God's response to Phinehas' action is telling. In Numbers 25:10–13, God makes a covenant of peace with him, promising that he and his descendants would always have a place in His service. God states,

> *"Phinehas, son of Eleazar, the son of Aaron, has turned my anger away from the Israelites. Since he was as zealous for my honor among them as I am, I did not put an end to them in my zeal."*

Phinehas' story teaches us that zeal for God isn't just about fervor or enthusiasm; it's about taking God's commands seriously and upholding His honor. It challenges us to reflect on how our actions reflect our own zeal for God's honor, righteousness, and truth.

David

David, the shepherd boy who became Israel's greatest king, displayed an extraordinary zeal for God, setting a high standard for all believers. His passion for God's law, His house, and His righteousness illuminates the pages of the Psalms, demonstrating an exceptional example of fervor and dedication to God.

O God, You know my foolishness; And my sins are not hidden from You. ⁶ Let not those who wait for You, O Lord God of hosts, be ashamed because of me; Let not those who seek You be confounded because of me, O God of Israel. ⁷ Because for Your sake I have borne reproach; Shame has covered my face. ⁸ I have become a stranger to my brothers, and an alien to my mother's children; ⁹ Because zeal for Your house has eaten me up, And the reproaches of those who reproach You have fallen on me. ¹⁰ When I wept and chastened my soul with fasting, That became my reproach. ¹¹ I also made sackcloth my garment; I became a byword to them. ¹² Those who sit in the gate speak against me, And I am the song of the drunkards. ¹³ But as for me, my prayer is to You, O Lord, in the acceptable time; O God, in the multitude of Your mercy, Hear me in the truth of Your Salvation. Psalm 69:5-13

Here in Psalm 69:5-13, David's zeal for God's house is evident. He speaks of the reproaches that have fallen upon him for the sake of God. David, the anointed King, is not concerned with his personal reputation or the scorn he faces from others, even his own family. His preoccupation, instead, is with God's honor.

The Psalm says, "zeal for Your house has eaten me up," depicting David's intense devotion to God. His love for God and His house is so strong that it consumes him, leading him to bear reproach, endure shame, and isolate himself from his family and society.

Another example of David's zeal for God is found in Psalm 119:137-144

The Snare of Indifference

Righteous are You, O Lord, And upright are Your judgments. 138 Your testimonies, which You have commanded, Are righteous and very faithful. 139 My zeal has consumed me, Because my enemies have forgotten Your words. 140 Your word is very pure; Therefore Your servant loves it. 141 I am small and despised, Yet I do not forget Your precepts. 142 Your righteousness is an everlasting righteousness, And Your law is truth. 143 Trouble and anguish have overtaken me, Yet Your commandments are my delights. 144 The righteousness of Your testimonies is everlasting; Give me understanding, and I shall live.

David's zeal for God is not just focused on His house but also extends to His words and commandments. As we see in Psalm 119:137-144, David's passion for God's law is so immense that he states, "My zeal has consumed me, Because my enemies have forgotten Your words."

Despite his own struggles and the contempt of his enemies, David clings to God's commandments, finding delight in them even amidst trouble and anguish. His love for God's word is so intense that it outweighs the derision and hardship he faces.

Furthermore, David's fervor does not only express itself in devotion and adherence to God's laws but also in prayer. His earnest plea to God in Psalm 69:13, "But as for me, my prayer is to You, O LORD, in the acceptable time," reveals his dependence on God and commitment to seeking God's face, regardless of his circumstances.

David's zeal for God—displayed in his respect for God's house, his love for God's word, and his fervent prayers—is not a transient or superficial enthusiasm but a deep, abiding passion that guided his actions and formed the bedrock of his relationship with God.

As such, David stands as a powerful example for all believers, challenging us to examine our own lives and consider how our zeal for God manifests in our love for His house, His word, and our prayer life.

Elijah

Elijah, often referred to as "the prophet of fire," was one of the most fiery and zealous prophets of the Old Testament. His life, detailed in the books of 1 and 2 Kings, was filled with dramatic moments as he fearlessly stood up for the Lord against King Ahab and the prophets of Baal, exhibiting an exceptional zeal for God.

The events recorded in 1 Kings 16 through 18 reveal the zeal of Elijah in action. Against King Ahab, who built an altar in the temple of Baal, Elijah warned of a severe drought as a divine punishment for worshipping false gods (1 Kings 17:1).

This episode showcases Elijah's boldness in delivering God's message despite the king's blatant disregard for the Lord's commandments. His fervor for God is evident in his willingness to speak truth to power, even at significant personal risk.

Elijah's interactions with the widow of Sidon further illustrate his zeal. Guided by God, he traveled to Sidon, where he miraculously brought the widow's dead son back to life (1 Kings 17:17-23). Despite being a stranger in a foreign land, Elijah's devotion to God's work was unwavering.

Perhaps the most remarkable demonstration of Elijah's fervor was his confrontation with the prophets of Baal on

Mount Carmel. This event, recorded in 1 Kings 18:19-39, showcased God's supremacy when He answered Elijah's prayer with fire from heaven, proving His might to the people and vindicating Elijah's faith.

However, being zealous for God did not spare Elijah from human fears and anxieties. After all these miraculous victories, Elijah found himself fleeing from Jezebel's wrath, expressing feelings of despair and isolation as we read in 1 Kings 19:9-13:

> *⁹ And there he went into a cave, and spent the night in that place; and behold, the word of the Lord came to him, and He said to him, "What are you doing here, Elijah?" ¹⁰ So he said, "I have been very zealous for the Lord God of hosts; for the children of Israel have forsaken Your covenant, torn down Your altars, and killed Your prophets with the sword. I alone am left; and they seek to take my life." ¹¹Then He said, "Go out, and stand on the mountain before the Lord." And behold, the Lord passed by, and a great and strong wind tore into the mountains and broke the rocks in pieces before the Lord, but the Lord was not in the wind; and after the wind an earthquake, but the Lord was not in the earthquake;¹² and after the earthquake a fire, but the Lord was not in the fire; and after the fire a still small voice. ¹³So it was, when Elijah heard it, that he wrapped his face in his mantle and went out and stood in the entrance of the cave.*

Notice how even in moments of vulnerability, Elijah's zeal for God remained central to his identity, serving as a driving force that guided his actions.

Elijah's life underscores that walking in zeal for the Lord does not equate to a life devoid of trials and tribulations.

Instead, it often involves boldness, faith, resilience, and an unwavering commitment to God's commandments, even in the face of seemingly insurmountable challenges.

By following the example set by zealous individuals like Elijah, we can also cultivate an enduring passion for God, leading lives that honor Him, no matter what circumstances we face.

Jeremiah

Jeremiah, known as the "weeping prophet," was a man who embodied a remarkable zeal for God despite facing continual opposition, persecution, and derision.

His zeal for God was not marked by triumphant victories or miraculous signs, as seen in the lives of Phinehas, David, and Elijah, but rather by his unyielding dedication to God's message amidst harsh trials as we see in Jeremiah 20:7-10:

> O Lord, You induced me, and I was persuaded; You are stronger than I, and have prevailed. I am in derision daily; Everyone mocks me. *8* For when I spoke, I cried out; I shouted, "Violence and plunder!" Because the word of the Lord was made to me A reproach and a derision daily. *9* Then I said, "I will not make mention of Him, Nor speak anymore in His name." But His word was in my heart like a burning fire Shut up in my bones; I was weary of holding it back, And I could not. *10* For I heard many mocking: "Fear on every side!" "Report," they say, "and we will report it!" All my acquaintances watched for my stumbling, saying, "Perhaps he can be induced; Then we will prevail against him, And we will take our revenge on him."

In these verses, we see Jeremiah's intimate, raw confession, expressing his innermost feelings about the daunting task he had been called to. Jeremiah's mission was to proclaim a message of impending judgment, violence, and plunder - a message that was not welcomed by his contemporaries and resulted in his ridicule and mockery.

Despite the immense pressure, Jeremiah remained committed to God's call. His words in verse 9, "But His word was in my heart like a burning fire Shut up in my bones; I was weary of holding it back, And I could not," encapsulate his overwhelming zeal for the Lord. Even though he considered ceasing to speak God's words, he found it impossible to keep silent. The word of God was like a fire in his heart and bones, compelling him to continue despite the backlash he received.

The constant mockery, derision, and threats to Jeremiah's life did not extinguish his fervor. Instead, they further revealed his dedication and steadfastness in the face of adversity. Despite knowing the cost, he remained faithful to his divine mission.

Jeremiah's life offers a powerful example of zeal for God that perseveres through hardship. His story demonstrates that genuine zeal for God doesn't guarantee comfort or ease. Sometimes, it may lead to misunderstanding, rejection, and persecution. Yet, like Jeremiah, those zealous for the Lord continue to serve Him, driven by a divine fire that cannot be quenched and empowered by God's strength amid adversity.

Esther

Esther, a Jewish girl who had become the queen of Persia under King Ahasuerus (also known as King Xerxes), is a perfect embodiment of what it means to have a zealous love for God and His people.

The story of Esther is unique in the Bible, not only for its dramatic twists and turns but also because it doesn't explicitly mention God. Yet, God's hand is evident throughout Esther's life and the preservation of the Jewish people.

The situation arose when Haman, a high-ranking official in the king's court and the story's antagonist, convinced the king to issue a decree to annihilate all the Jews in the kingdom out of his personal vendetta against Esther's cousin, Mordecai.

When Mordecai learns of this plan, he sends a message to Esther, pleading with her to go to the king and beg for the lives of her people.

Esther was in a precarious situation. To approach the king unsummoned was a crime punishable by death unless the king extended his golden scepter as a sign of mercy. Moreover, Esther had hidden her Jewish identity. She had to reveal this secret to plead for her people, not knowing how the king would react.

Queen Esther demonstrated her profound faith and reliance on God in this dire situation. She asked Mordecai to gather all the Jews in the capital city of Susa and join her in a three-day fast before she would dare to go before the king (Esther 4:16). Her words, "And if I perish, I perish," attest to the depth of her commitment and her zeal for God's people.

After three days, Esther approached the king, and by God's grace, he extended his scepter, sparing her life. Then, through a series of divinely orchestrated events, Esther revealed Haman's wicked plot, leading to Haman's execution and the issuance of a new decree allowing the Jews to defend themselves against their enemies.

Esther's faith and courage in the face of danger show her profound trust in God. Her willingness to risk her life for the welfare of God's people demonstrates a zeal beyond her personal safety and comfort.

Mary

Mary, the mother of Jesus, is an inspiring example of zeal for God in the Bible. Though a young, betrothed woman living in a society that placed great importance on appearances and public honor, she exhibited remarkable faith when faced with the angel Gabriel's announcement that she was chosen to conceive God's Son.

In the annunciation narrative in the Gospel of Luke, the angel Gabriel visits Mary and proclaims, "Greetings, you who are highly favored! The Lord is with you" (Luke 1:28).

Mary was greatly troubled by his words, but Gabriel comforted her, explaining that she would conceive and give birth to a Son, Jesus, who would be called the Son of the Most High (Luke 1:31-33).

Such news could have been overwhelming. In those times, the implications of being pregnant while unmarried were severe, including public disgrace, rejection by family and community, and even the possibility of being stoned to death.

Mary had every reason to fear and decline. However, her response to this daunting news was, "I am the Lord's servant... may your word to me be fulfilled" (Luke 1:38).

Her acceptance of God's plan, despite the potential repercussions, reflected her incredible zeal for God and her complete trust in His providence.

This spirit of obedience and faith continued throughout her life. Mary followed Jesus during His ministry, was present at the foot of the cross when He was crucified, and after His ascension, she was with the apostles in the upper room, participating in prayer and the early life of the Church (Acts 1:14).

Mary's zeal for God led her to say yes to the extraordinary, to accept a responsibility far beyond her own strength and understanding. Her journey was not easy, marked by significant trials and heartbreaks, but her unwavering faith and commitment to God's will are a testament to her zeal.

Jesus Christ

Jesus Christ, our perfect exemplar, showed an unrivaled zeal for the Lord. Unlike many others, His zeal wasn't just about obedience to religious regulations or performing great miracles, although He certainly did those things.

Instead, Jesus demonstrated a zeal born out of a profound love for God and a deep commitment to upholding the sanctity and honor of God's dwelling place.

One example of Jesus' zeal is found in John 2:13-17:

> *13 Now the Passover of the Jews was at hand, and Jesus went up to Jerusalem. 14 And He found in the temple those who sold oxen and sheep and doves, and the money changers doing business. 15 When He had made a whip of cords, He drove them all out of the temple, with the sheep and the oxen, and poured out the changers' money and overturned the tables. 16 And He said*

to those who sold doves, "Take these things away! Do not make My Father's house a house of merchandise!" ¹⁷ *Then His disciples remembered that it was written, "Zeal for Your house has eaten Me up."*

This passage reveals a vivid incident where Jesus's zeal was manifested in an intense act of cleansing the temple. The scene was Jerusalem during the time of the Passover, a holy period for the Jewish people.

Yet, instead of reverence, Jesus found a commercial scene in the temple with traders selling oxen, sheep, and doves, and money changers carrying out business transactions.

In a display of righteous indignation, Jesus crafted a whip of cords and expelled all the traders from the temple, overturning their tables and pouring out their ill-gained money. His words, "Take these things away! Do not make My Father's house a house of merchandise!" echoed through the temple court, a testament to His zeal for the purity and sanctity of God's house.

His disciples later recollected the scriptural phrase, "Zeal for Your house has eaten Me up," recognizing its fulfillment in Jesus' actions that day. This phrase paints a vivid picture of Jesus' fervor. His zeal was so intense; it consumed Him, motivating His actions and guiding His path.

Jesus' zeal led Him not only to teach and heal but also to confront and correct the wrong. It wasn't driven by anger or personal pride but came from His deep love for God and commitment to upholding His honor. His life, teachings, and actions give us the ultimate example of what it truly means to walk in zeal for the Lord.

Paul

The apostle Paul is another powerful example of the transformation that comes when zeal is aligned with the truth of Christ. In his former life as Saul of Tarsus, Paul was characterized by his remarkable zeal, albeit misplaced, as he actively persecuted the early Christian Church.

He passionately sought to extinguish the fledgling faith, even to the extent of consenting to the martyrdom of Stephen, the first Christian martyr (Acts 8:1).

But the radical encounter with Jesus Christ on the road to Damascus transformed Paul's life and redirected his zeal. His fervor, once used for persecuting the Church, was now employed in its propagation. Paul's new-found zeal was evidenced in his tireless mission work, spreading the gospel across the Roman Empire, establishing churches, and mentoring new believers (Romans 15:20).

He warned against false teachers who showed a manipulative kind of zeal aimed at misleading others (Galatians 4:17).

In Romans 9:1-5, we glimpse the depth and intensity of Paul's zeal after his conversion.

> *I tell the truth in Christ, I am not lying, my conscience also bearing me witness in the Holy Spirit, ² that I have great sorrow and continual grief in my heart. ³ For I could wish that I myself were accursed from Christ for my brethren, my countrymen according to the flesh, ⁴ who are Israelites, to whom pertain the adoption, the glory, the covenants, the giving of the law, the service of God, and the promises; ⁵ of whom are the fathers and*

from whom, according to the flesh, Christ came, who is over all, the eternally blessed God. Amen.

In this scripture, Paul expresses deep sorrow and unceasing anguish for his fellow Israelites, who, despite their privileged position as God's chosen people, failed to recognize Jesus as the Messiah.

His zeal for their salvation was so intense that he could wish himself accursed, cut off from Christ if it could secure their salvation. This is a radical expression of self-sacrificial love and an example of the zealous heart fueled by Christ's love.

Such was the zealous fervor of Paul. From a fervent persecutor to a passionate proclaimer, Paul's life serves as an example of the transformative power of the Gospel and the profound impact of a heart aflame with zeal for God's glory and the advancement of His kingdom.

Cultivating Zeal for God

Zeal for the Lord starkly contrasts the perils of spiritual apathy or lukewarmness. As we navigate through these end times, a resurgence of this fervor, this divine passion, is an essential part of our spiritual armor.

Our commitment should not wane but rather intensify in serving Jesus and communicating the gospel's transformative power to others (Matthew 28:18–19; Romans 3:24).

The Baptism of the Holy Spirit, a pivotal experience in our Christian journey, is designed to produce something other than passive or tepid followers of Christ.

Quite the contrary, it ignites a fire within us, cultivating fervent disciples of Jesus Christ. These empowered individuals are credible witnesses of the Word Made Flesh, stirring their surroundings and inspiring others to embrace the saving grace of Jesus.

As New Testament believers, we are given a clear directive in Romans 12:11: "Never be lacking in zeal, but keep your spiritual fervor, serving the Lord." This zealous disposition is not simply an added bonus but a fundamental trait in our relationship with God, our spiritual lives, and participation in His kingdom work.

Unfortunately, in our quest for worldly wisdom and sophistication, some Christians have allowed their spiritual fervor to cool, even in the face of apparent evil.

But let us evaluate ourselves critically. Is our approach genuinely reflective of the wisdom from above, or have we slipped into a state of lukewarmness - a dangerous complacency or indifference towards the things of God?

Therefore, let us stoke the fires of our faith, nurturing a spirit of zeal that fuels our love for God and our passion for His kingdom. Our world desperately needs those who, undeterred by the challenges of the times, embody the burning zeal of the Lord in every facet of their lives.

Remember, our zeal is not just about us; it's about demonstrating God's love to a needy world. So, let's make sure our spiritual temperature is set to 'hot.'

Epilogue

Wilt thou not revive us again: That thy people may rejoice in thee? Psalms 85:6

As I put down my pen, I reflect on our journey together through these pages, guided by an enduring passion that burns within my heart.

That passion is fueled by an earnest longing for the readiness of every believer for the imminent return of the Lord—the rapture.

It is an era of confusion and tumult, with the Church standing at its epicenter. The sacred halls of Christianity, unfortunately, are not immune to the pervasive influence of worldly philosophies and ideologies.

False teachings seep through the cracks like an insidious fog, while self-proclaimed prophets weave webs of deception, leading many astray.

Such disturbances have shaken the faith of some to its very

core, with despair causing them to abandon their Christian faith entirely. Meanwhile, the actions of certain high-profile Christian leaders, far from edifying the body, have sown seeds of doubt and disillusionment.

We must acknowledge that these leaders, like all of us, are human and susceptible to error. However, the consequences of their actions remain profoundly damaging.

With each passing day, it becomes painfully apparent that the sensitivity and alertness to the Second Coming of Jesus Christ that was characteristic of the early church has been blunted in many believers today.

This book, then, is more than just a manuscript—it is a clarion call. A call to awaken, to rekindle the fervent love we once had for the Lord in the early days of our rebirth.

It is a summons to shake off the dust that has gathered on our faith and to break free from the icy chains of lukewarmness that have ensnared us.

My heartfelt prayer as we close this book is for us to reclaim our zealous faith in Christ and commit ourselves to the diligent maintenance of true spirituality in Christ.

With God's help, let us strive to ensure that the flame of our faith never flickers but burns ever brightly, illuminating the path for those who might otherwise be lost in the gathering gloom.

As the dawn of His coming draws ever closer, may we stand as beacons of His love, His truth, and His promise, fervently aflame with zeal for His glorious kingdom.

The Snare of Indifference

O LORD, I have heard thy speech, and was afraid: O LORD, revive thy work in the midst of the years, in the midst of the years make known; in wrath remember mercy. Habakkuk 3:2

So help us, God.

About the Author

With over four decades of Ministry behind him, Archbishop Nicholas Duncan-Williams is the Presiding Archbishop and General Overseer of Action Chapel International (ACI), headquartered in Accra, Ghana, and United Denominations of Action Chapel International, which has over 150 affiliates and branch churches located in North America, Europe, Asia, and Africa.

Archbishop Duncan-Williams is also the Founder and Chairman of Nicholas Duncan-Williams Ministries (formerly Prayer Summit International), which hosts prayer summits around the globe, bringing revival to international cities through corporate and intercessory prayer and training.

With a unique anointing in prayer and intercession, Archbishop is recognized by many leaders in the body of Christ as the "Apostle of Strategic Prayer."

Having gained accreditation and respect from recognized church leaders, God has used him to counsel and speak into the lives of world leaders while still maintaining his touch with the everyday person. As a result, he is affectionately called "Papa" by many.

When you join One Million Strong, you will gain instant access to:

- **Financial Freedom Prayer Declaration**
- **Discover the Secrets to Effective Prayer** Course
- **Breakthrough in the Spiritual Realm** Audio

Made in the USA
Middletown, DE
08 July 2024

56905175R00071